# SEVEN POWERFUL STRATEGIES TO ACCELERATE YOUR BUSINESS

IF YOU ARE LEADING A BUSINESS in today's turbulent global markets, you know the drill. Compared to many of the international behemoths roaming the world, you may have limited resources, shallower pockets, fewer in-house MBAs, and personally more at risk. You understand what lonely at the top means.

*Beneath the Armor* identifies seven strategies defined by your most successful peers that will provide you a roadmap to overcome your possible isolation and scarcity of assets. Implementing the seven strategies will position you at eye-level with your worldwide, giant competitors.

The strategies are simple, relevant, and within your capabilities to implement. Attempting to apply the various doctrines and strategies of the big business tycoons may have been frustrating. Not any longer. Finally, you have a book that is dedicated to addressing your specific needs and situation.

# BENEATH THE
# ARMOR

# BENEATH THE
# ARMOR

*How Business Leaders
Stand Tall in a Turbulent
Global Economy*

OLE CARLSON

Library of Congress No.: 2003099761
ISBN: 0-9766705-1-8

This book was printed in the United States of America.

Published by Influencemany

To order additional copies of this book, contact
**www.influencemany.com**

# CONTENTS

# DEDICATION

*Beneath the Armor* is dedicated to those business leaders who occupy the top slot on the organization chart. The message in this book comes from you and your peers and I am simply paying it forward.

Above all, I dedicate this work to my love, Sue Ann. She entered my life to assist me in discovering who I really am, to envelop me in unconditional love, and to play with me like I have never played before.

# ACKNOWLEDGMENTS

*"Beneath the flimflam of the Christmas letter
lurks the heart of a legitimate writer."*
—AL LIBKE

AL IS A FRATERNITY BROTHER, friend, and physician. Those words were scribbled on the back of a returned Christmas letter that I had mailed to friends and family in the late 1960s. The message has haunted me for decades. Al, I am sorry it took almost 35 years, but here it is.

One more person, among scores of others who influenced my path, needs to be acknowledged. Jim Jensen, entrepreneur, CEO, and mentor, entered my life at a time when I was wandering and offered me an opportunity and vision of myself that seemed out of reach. It was not. I shall always be grateful. Jim started me on my journey of exploration, success, and doing what I was meant to do and being who I was meant to be.

# INTRODUCTION

*"Getting an idea should be like sitting on a pin.*
*It should make you jump up and do something."*
—E.L. Simpson

IN A RECENT NETWORK TELEVISION COMMERCIAL, two, buttoned-down, pinstripe business consultants are sitting across the immaculate desk of an interested and attentive CEO. A comprehensive and apparently costly new re-engineering approach for the CEO's business is being proposed by the advisors and thoughtfully considered by the corporate leader. When the recommendation is concluded, the CEO nods favorably toward them and says, "This looks fantastic. When can you get started?"

The two advisors quickly exchange astonished glances. One of the experts, eyebrows slightly arching and failing to conceal an emerging smirk, replies to the CEO, "We don't actually *do* what we propose." Momentum stalling silence follows.

The scene concludes with the consultants walking through the building's lobby, embossed leather briefcases swinging, heads shaking side to side, with one softly muttering to the other, "I can't believe he actually expected us to *do* the work. What's with that guy?"

If you are the leader of a business, this is all-too-familiar territory. Consultants, board members, professional service providers, and a vast assortment of others outside the walls and borders of your organization are willing to volunteer suggestions on how you should lead and manage your business. When the lights are off, however, and everyone except you has gone to the comforts of home, it all comes to a sobering and tire screeching halt. You are usually left with the doing. It is your time, your money, your energy, and your expertise that you draw upon while the external advisors circle the perimeter and gaze critically inward through the corporate windows.

Most of you have not corralled a herd of MBAs stationed down the hall to launch state-of-the-art strategies as Jack Welch did and could. You know at a subatomic particle level what "lonely at the top" implies. Welcome to the intersection where the buck either stops or is handed to others.

What do you do? Here is what. Read and constantly reference *Beneath the Armor*. Deliberately tap into the triumphant real-life, real-time, and real-money knowledge of honorable leaders pulling long oars similar to yours. Learn what other highly effective leaders have done to accelerate to the next level of their business and soar skyward on their individual and professional journey. Most of you have been at the helm of your businesses with a high courage, low-to-medium competency model. It was what many of you had to do to get to your present station. You are the only one who can boost the courage quotient if it is in your DNA. What can be increased, with my assistance, is your leadership competency (if you are willing).

By purchasing and reading this book, I assume that you want to be more successful doing what you do. I have encountered those of you who are frustrated by reading the volumes of best-selling business books authored by the giants of the international business world when you do not have the resources that they all possess. I know many of you who are embarrassed and indignant about being associated with the high profile, get rich-by-any-means, business leaders who crowd today's police beat headlines.

Can you honestly relate to what the tycoons are doing relative to your unique circumstances? Are you tired of faddish, philosophical, and ever-changing academic approaches to leading a successful enterprise? Do you hunger for a resource that is relevant, congruent, and calibrates with what you are dealing with day to day? If I am on target and hitting an exposed nerve, keep turning the pages.

*Beneath the Armor* springs from multiple wells. For nearly two decades, I have worked exclusively with owners, CEOs, and presidents of all sorts and sizes of prospering businesses. I have spent in excess of 16,000 hours facilitating CEO group meetings, teaching strategy workshops, and participating in one-on-one coaching sessions with thousands of successful corporate heads. My role has been as an advocate, teacher, facilitator, challenger, conscience, consultant, friend, counselor, and occasionally a pain in the butt. These meetings, workshops, and conversations, took place month after month, year after year, enabling me to witness firsthand what business leaders confronted, what was considered, what was implemented, and what actually worked. It was real life, in real time, risking and spending real money, with real get-your-attention consequences. It was, as Dr. Phil would say, the real deal.

I stood shoulder to shoulder with executives witnessing the agony of executing a downsizing, firing a chronic under-performing employee, making payroll periodically with personal credit cards, or sheepishly borrowing, once again, from ageing parents or in-laws. I was present watching leaders stumble into the office, exhausted after sleeping on a hard pillow all night worrying about losing a key customer, having a bank note immediately called, or facing a difficult, gut-wrenching conversation with a poorly performing direct report. I celebrated with my clients when they triumphed over impending behemoth competitors or handed out size-able bonus checks. I understood deeply their pride when ushering a company tour exhibiting to prospective cus-tomers what they had created, and what they could offer. I was present, entrenched in a front line foxhole, armed and dangerous, learning what worked for the client beside me.

My clients and I had the opportunity to participate in monthly three-hour business seminars conducted by experts who were current on every imaginable business and person-al growth topic. Curriculum from these workshops filled my professional and private toolbox with fresh perspectives and potent actions to explore with clients. I had my own live, in-the-moment, business and personal growth laboratory, testing processes, strategies, and tactics while measuring observable results.

I have conducted more than 500 interactive strategic busi-ness seminars with CEO audiences in the United States, United Kingdom, Ireland, France, Holland, Canada, Mexico, and Australia. The agendas dealt with innovative leadership ideas and proven best practices. My clients and I gained enormously by exploring and applying the material from these workshops.

*Beneath the Armor* reveals seven potent, irrefutable business strategies to rocket boost your business forward and upward. The strategies originate from business leaders who have been there and done that. Never mind rewarding them with a simple T-shirt, they deserve the latest that Armani has to offer. Their fingerprints, footprints, and dental records are all over the following chapters. You do not need to invent anything. It is always easier to imitate with your own spin rather than initiate. You do not need to think and act out of the box. Implement in your own individual style. Do not assume that you know these strategies or are currently executing them at the highest level. I did the heavy lifting and sorting. I isolated and simplified the significant seven because they are valid, relevant, and will calibrate with you and with what I believe most of you are trying to do with your businesses.

Be careful not to discount the first blush simplicity of what is being suggested in this book. It has been my experience working with business leaders, that there is a desire to believe there is and to discover the silver bullet; to finally and ultimately be told the "exact truth" about how to succeed in your business. Forget that notion. Sorry, it is not going to happen in your lifetime. Too many of you are more than willing and much too eager to place your faith in and subordinate your experience to expert advice. Remember, nobody cares about or understands your business better than you.

Authors and consultants are willing and anxious to suggest that they have the "magic sauce" that provides the definitive ingredients to your ultimate success. In the past, publishers have subjected you to *Total Quality Management, Re-engineering, Open Book Management, Quality Circles, Empowerment, Excellence and Award Programs, 360 Degree Feedback Encounters, Top Down, Bottom Up, Learning Organizations,* and countless other sophisticated business disciplines designed to tune, shape, and sharpen your business. The business and diet books just keep on coming. They create a predictable and constant revenue stream for the authors, agents, and publishing houses. The bombardment is overwhelming and much too confusing. You cannot afford to have your employees chronically confused and wondering what the next answer is going to be as they roll into their parking stall on Monday morning. Let these business flavors of the month flow by as a bubbling brook, and every once in awhile, when a piece of the offering appears to fit and is appropriate for you and your business, dip your net into the passing stream and fish out that element of the program that works for you and your individual style. There is no one way to be successful.

You can rely on my research and experience with thousands of victorious leaders and my ability to pass on to you what really works and what does not. I am the conduit and the channel to your peers who have defined a pathway to being successful. The direction and caution signs have been carefully put in place.

Be mindful that in the past many of you have only had you and your immediate inner circle. That is your limitation and perhaps a potentially foul-smelling albatross hanging around your neck. You do not have to lead all alone. I am exposing you to thousands of success stories showing you a well-groomed trail. Your colleagues are providing you stable training wheels.

I am your personal valet helping you to suit up, arming you with the seven strategies, and preparing you for your next joust in this global business environment. The shield is in place. Begin immediately. No need to wait, but please not all seven strategies at once. Be patient (I know that's not in your DNA). Keep in mind most of you have done fine up to this juncture and here is a little help.

*Beneath the Armor* will inspire you to:

- **Come out from behind your corporate mask and be truly authentic.**

- **Take better care of yourself.**

- **Lead the organization effectively.**

- **Overcome adversity and setbacks.**

- **Develop and leverage the talent in your organization.**

- **Understand the importance of being financially healthy.**

- **Remain flexible and responsive to changing business environments.**

This book is not a passive reading experience with you lounging in front of a crackling fire, feet up on the burgundy leather recliner, slowly sipping an exalted 2000 vintage Bordeaux. You have recipes to learn and cooking to do.

Employees are going to show up shortly and they are hungry for your leadership. The learning is generative and consumptive, rich and plentiful. Grab your highlighter and laptop. Approach this information as if it really mattered. It does. It ought to. This plate is where the majority of your meat and potatoes lie, where your net worth resides, where you spend most of your time, what drains or jumpstarts your energy, what engages your emotions, your intellect, and ultimately makes uncompromising demands on your physical, emotional, and psychological well-being. You and I are members of the tribe who truly understand the conditions under which you live.

Each chapter concludes with you participating in exercises and journal work anchoring the strategies and propelling you beyond where you are currently stationed. Participate. Demand deliberate and intentional action from yourself rather than settling for an intellectual understanding of the material.

There are new frontiers for you to explore, new markets and segments to penetrate. The business deserves your absolute utmost attention to meet the needs and demands of your employees, customers, family, and most important, yourself. I insist that your personal and professional life be easier, more prosperous, more joyful, more fulfilling, and more in balance. It is important that you value yourself as much as I do. I am one of your most devoted and attentive advocates and want you to sweep a staggering stack of chips off the table when you have arrived at your knowing when to hold 'em and when to fold 'em crossroads. Understanding and implementing these strategies will speed you to where you desire and deserve to go.

You have arrived at an important intersection of your professional and personal life. They are inseparable for most of you. "Don't take it personally, it's only business," is a line that is appropriate and plays well in Mafia movies but not in real life when your future is on the line. Business is always personal when you are the leader. By reading *Beneath the Armor*, you have demonstrated a commitment to become better at what you do. You have dedicated yourself to be more successful, to reach your full potential, to not settle, and to be more accountable. As my Australian friends would say, "Good on you."

At the 1993 ESPY awards on ESPN, a bone cancer-stricken Jim Valvano, then the coach of the highly successful North Carolina State basketball team, was assisted to the podium by ushers to address an audience of his coaching peers, broadcasters, world-class athletes, and writers. He had only a limited number of days to live. In an impassioned speech, he shared his formula for living a productive and fulfilled life. In a weakened but inspired voice, he said you must "never give up." In addition, you must do the following everyday:

◆ **You must laugh.**

◆ **You must think.**

◆ **You must have an experience that moves your emotions to tears.**

He went on to say that if you can laugh, think, and cry everyday that you have had a heck of a day.

I hope that you have that experience reading this book and leading your company, that every chapter in this book and every day at work provides you the opportunity to laugh at your circumstances, think profound thoughts, and shed a few tears. Now, that would be a heck of a read and a heck of a day at the office. Also, to never give up.

Now, get busy. Cling firmly to what works for you. Ride it for all it is worth. Discard what has become habitual, comfortable, or familiar but no longer serves you and the organization as it did in the past. It is a brand-new day that is going to be much different from yesterday and tomorrow much different from today. The velocity of change and impending world competition is accelerating. There are predators outside your company door capturing your market share, pursuing your clients, and seducing your key employees.

Wear your suit of armor well. Execute the seven strategies to the max as you stride out into today's high velocity business environment. I wish you good fortune. Stand tall.

# 1

## STRATEGY ONE:
## Be Authentic—It is Easier to Remember

*It's not easy being green.*
—KERMIT THE FROG

∽

**Be who you are and not whom you
think you should be.**

PEOPLE CONSTRUCT VARIOUS PERSONAS throughout
their lifetime to create a desired impression on any given
audience perhaps securing a safe and familiar base camp. At
times, these contrived and constructed personalities serve us
well by providing protection and sanctuaries, fixing what we
need at that moment, or allowing us to pass through a difficult period with as few emotional, psychological, and
physical abrasions as possible. For many, the different characters and roles we assume are vital and essential survival
mechanisms providing temporary shelter and predictability
as we journey through our life. As spiritual writer Deepak
Chopra suggests, "There are many personalities competing
for the use of your body."

Some of the roles we choose are consciously scripted. Others are unconscious or bioreactive missiles automatically launched in a split second from deeply embedded silos buried in our psyche and triggered by a need for flight, fight, freeze, or appease. The danger lies in the personalities being inappropriate or implementing strategies and stories that no longer serve us or others well. It has been said, "When the horse is dead get off." It is good advice, especially if you are the leader of an organization performing in front of varied internal, external, and critical audiences.

While in college, I had a variety of looks and behaviors depending upon where I was, whom I was with, and what I was doing. The "party animal" role differed greatly from the "going to a fraternity brother's parent's home for dinner" guise. Occasionally the bewildered "deer in the headlights" exterior came out when I was clueless and did not know what to say or how to behave. Perhaps in those instances, I was most genuine, most authentic.

I have observed many CEOs wearing a variety of masks depending upon their circumstances. It must be confusing to the people who are consistently with them in those various occasions. "Hey boss, customer, vendor, friend, spouse, parent, just who are you, really?"

Often, I felt like an impostor; the deceptive pretender unsure that what I had to offer would suffice, would work, and be acceptable in particular situations. Many of you deal in business with the imposter syndrome. You know what I mean. What would happen if my employees, my board, and my partner, find out that I am making this up as I go along?

What if all those people discover my frailties and insecurities? Will they still follow and believe in me?

My journey to authenticity and self-acceptance was long and at times terrifying. It had unanticipated starts and stops, often seasoned with excitement and despair. There was acceptance and rejection, ultimately covering the full range of the human experience. Self-discovery is a recommended passage for business leaders to eventually realize and ultimately accept who they really are and what they have become. Warning, you had better buckle your safety belt low and tight across your lap because there can be some unanticipated turbulence along the way.

One of my early personalities was the role I fabricated as a copier salesperson for the Xerox Corporation. Fresh out of university, with a liberal arts degree fluttering in hand, I convinced Xerox's Northwest Regional branch manager to turn me loose in downtown Seattle peddling copiers and supplies. I had zero business experience but the people I observed in liberal arts were not setting the financial world on fire and I wanted the prosperity and the good life that the business world seemingly offered. I had my confident, I can do anything character locked in forward gear.

To create this new and unfamiliar business image, I purchased four single-breasted inexpensive wool suits from a two-for-one university district college clothier, bought a synthetic leather briefcase, polished my scuffed fraternity issue brown wingtips, and scampered out to take head-on 3M, AB Dick, and Thermo-Fax. Xerox was king. The Japanese had yet to enter the market.

On the first day, in a downtown business district territory, I scurried past a window display at a national department store. I was in a hurry to make my first sale. Slow down! It caught my eye, a black-and-gray houndstooth hat set on top of a frozen-faced male mannequin outfitted in the most current and fashionable Madison Avenue professional attire. Perfect...just what I needed to complete the look of what I perceived a high-rolling professional Xerox salesperson should project. It fit. I bought it.

Briskly and confidently, I strolled out of the store with my new cap perched on my head. I had a new look, a new attitude, and an expectation of immediate success. The hat was just the stimulating spark that I thought I needed to be successful in this new venture and role. It was not! Several weeks later, feeling utterly conspicuous and a bit disappointed, I scampered about my territory with limited success. I was doing things right but not doing the right things. I was making the sales calls, giving the Xerox pitch, selling features and benefits but not closing many deals. I was rigid, unsure of myself, and attempting to be true to an image that felt intuitively distant and entirely unrelated. I was an insecure counterfeit and thought maybe liberal arts (whatever that was) was not such a bad career to pursue after all.

The new business bonnet got in the way. I looked like a young Paul "Bear" Bryant minus a football team with only copiers and supplies to sell. Feeling utterly inadequate masquerading as an experienced, successful copier salesperson, I flopped and floundered in trying to be the whiz-bang sales hotshot that I thought I would automatically become by wearing that silly hat. I was memorizing, scripting, costuming, and pretending to be someone I never was or ever would be. I was a rigid, predictable robot long before robotics came onto assembly lines. Label me "Robo salesperson" stumbling my way through the steel and glass canyons of downtown Seattle.

Veteran Xerox salespeople snickered behind my back, and customers found the attire incongruent with the person standing before them. Transformation, I discovered painfully, was not an outside-in process, but rather an inside-out personal journey. Dressing up the exterior had little positive impact on the interior. The hat became a symbol of phoniness, and one day, it was forever banished to a basement closet, never to crown my head again.

The next four quarters, sans hat and sporting another new attitude, I reset the look and strategy. It was a "no brainer." If I had persisted on doing what I had been doing, I would be standing ten deep in an unemployment line wearing that silly cap shuffling along with the rest of the underachievers. I took a deep cleansing breath, reached far inside, and let Ole escape. Whooooooooosh. It was a scary and uneven evolution, but it eventually worked. At times, I felt and may have looked like a large inflated balloon with the air suddenly escaping, flying about in unpredictable directions, bumping into walls, and jettisoning about on no particular set course. Miraculously, I never ran out of air and unexpectedly led the Northwest Region for that period in total copier and supplies sales. I was the comeback poster-child salesperson of the year. My more experienced and sophisticated colleagues ceased their behind my back snickering after my sales manager publicly cut me a bonus check larger than anything I could have ever imagined, and more substantial than most of them had experienced in their careers. So there!

Bare headed, check and bank deposit slip firmly in hand, I discovered that the secret to my newly acclaimed business triumph was to simply be myself and forget about conforming to the stoic mannequin in the gray flannel suit and houndstooth hat. It was not who I was. It was a life-altering lesson for a 23-year-old rookie who did not know much about business but was learning a great deal about himself. As Judy Garland once said, "Always be a first-rate version of yourself, instead of a second-rate version of somebody else."

Internally, I had ambition, curiosity, a diligent work ethic, and an innocent naivety. Not imitating others proved to be the path to my success. What was already inside was sufficient and more accessible than ever-changing images to portray, costumes to wear, and scripts to recite. I learned that to be authentic and effective, I had to eliminate, not add, to be more of who I really was and less of whom I thought I should be. In retrospect, it seems so obvious.

I discovered joyfully and was quite relieved that one bona fide look would be sufficient and usher me safely and successfully through life. Much of what was required for this journey was to fully show up and stay conscious. Comedian Woody Allen was right, "80 percent of life is simply showing up." How elementary. Show up! The houndstooth and its accompanying contrived personality placed a lid on my potential and natural abilities. The Xerox hat became a sombrero to hide under and to unconsciously snooze beneath. What was essential was to be present, pay attention, and remain awake in a world that was consistently falling asleep.

It just might be a competitive advantage. It was my first lesson in being authentic, in being an original.

Through the years, I have witnessed numerous business leaders hide behind masks that did not particularly serve them well or represent who they really were. They were just as guilty and misguided as I was. Is that you behind there? Are you wearing the expression that your mother/father left you? Did this look come from a management book? Are you the personification of your college professor, or are you just making it up as you go along? Take stock. Something is working in your professional career by your being who you are. You are sitting in a seat that few occupy successfully. Congratulations! You are certainly not Jack Welch. You never have been, and there is a 100 percent chance that you never will be. You are just you, and that is enough. Being your authentic self is good.

## Bring your best self forward and change what is not working.

Let me be clear. I am not suggesting that "being yourself" gives you permission to be an authentic jerk. You know people who deliberately hide behind despicable behavior claiming that they were just being real. They were simply getting clutter off their chests and being candidly honest. Leaders justifying and rationalizing this kind of behavior can cause irreparable destruction to the culture and human spirit in the business. It is selfish, shameful, and cowardly. They may feel better but the wake they leave behind is an intolerable toxic tidal wave flooding the organization with damaged human currency. What they have unilaterally decided is to take a short-term gain (not controlling or being accountable for their destructive behavior) for a long-term loss (high turnover, low morale, obedient employees).

We all have some behaviors that we would like to eliminate as leaders. In a recent survey, several CEOs of major corporations were asked to identify what they did not like about themselves as leaders and would be better off by not having the behavior. CEO Kalkhoven of JDS Uniphase stated, "Lack of patience." Whitman of eBay said, "Try to do too much at once." Schaeffer of Wellpoint stated, "Never satisfied." Kozlowski of Tyco indicated, "I am too impulsive." United Technologies leader David declared "Can't relax." Lewis of The New York Times commented, "Wished that I were smarter." What is your dislike and what price are you paying for not diluting or eliminating behaviors that no longer serve you or the organization well?

Steve was a branch manager whom I consulted for in a manufacturing business. His owner hired me to help Steve improve his leadership abilities. He lacked a formal education; however, he was acutely streetwise and knew how and when to take care of himself. Self-interest this client understood fully. He had risen to an impressive position in the company by being in the right place at the right time. On occasion, proper timing and extraordinary luck does work. Steve had far exceeded his life's dreams and aspirations. He was making more money and had more authority than he ever thought possible. Life was good for Steve with a senior executive vice president title, a luxury import automobile, and a split-level suburban home bordering a lush, manicured fairway. Ah, the good life.

Steve was a bully in a polyester sports coat cloaked as the leader of six already successful salespeople who were generating sizable quarterly bonus checks for him and his family. With his gun cocked and loaded, a nervous finger on the hair trigger, and his salespeople in the crosshairs, Steve was ready and willing to put down anyone who threatened his newly found prosperity and status in life. Survival instincts had overtaken good sense.

On Monday mornings, somewhere around eight o'clock, Steve conducted the weekly sales meeting. I attended as an observer and a coach. They were dreadful, self-esteem eroding occasions. The gatherings were planned poorly, unproductive, and shamefully unprofessional. They were a platform for Steve to publicly belittle, embarrass, threaten, and harass his sales force. Steve held forth to his obedient browbeaten audience with no sustainable substance. The further the individual or team was from making quota and reaching their goals, the more destructive and frightened Steve became. He was not concerned about their individual success, only his mattered. What frightened Steve to the bone was how their performance might reflect negatively on him and potentially threaten his position with the company and his recently celebrated lifestyle. He was wholly focused on and totally immersed in himself. His sales team was either his escalator to further glory, or a ticket on the down elevator to his previous unsatisfactory blue-collar life.

Anything was fair game for this branch manager on those appalling Monday mornings. Nothing was sacred or off limits. Nothing! He assaulted and penetrated barriers that would horrify any human resources director or corporate labor lawyer. Discussions of sexual conquests, drinking excursions, off-color jokes, and other nonbusiness taboo topics sprinkled the Monday morning agendas.

I recall one meeting when he noticed that Dave, a recently hired salesperson, had an obvious case of halitosis. Protocol or basic decency might suggest that Steve address that situation off line. Not a chance! He bellowed out in full volume to Dave and to the rest of the startled Certs-chomping observers that "his new salesman's breath smelled like horseshit." Interesting feedback. Thanks for sharing. Welcome to Steve's rendition of professional sales development and leadership.

If events were not going the way he thought they should, he would explode spontaneously; his puffy jowls suddenly expanding like a blowfish, his furrowing forehead turning various shades of scarlet, his darting eyes narrowed and penetrating, his mouth spewing spittle-laced profanity. He shouted, pounded his stubby fist on the table, sputtering and stumbling over a limited and crude vocabulary. Eventually, when the eruption had subsided and his sales force were frozen into solid lava, he would terminate the meeting by demanding that everyone get back to work and "Close some damn sales or else." Not exactly an effective or inspiring way to launch a sales team for the week.

The dictum was too late. The tsunami had moved inland. Foundations had been washed away and solid structures uprooted. The mudslide was moving. Steve felt great. He suggested that it was a "Terrific meeting. Don't you all agree?" It was all off his ample, self-serving chest. He viewed himself as a straight shooter who told it like it was. Steve wanted real men on his sales team. He was not like Jack Nicholson in the movie, *A Few Good Men,* who had assumed that Tom Cruise "couldn't handle the truth." He obviously thought that they could deal with anything that he put forth. In reality, they were not behaving like real men and handling Steve's offerings. Instead, they were silently limping off to their safe havens away from the office or behind tightly closed doors in private sanctuaries where they dealt with the humiliation in their own manner.

Collectively, they were a disservice to Steve. Nobody on that sales team confronted him on his style or his behavior. No one was willing to come forward and express the negative impact that his leadership was having on the organization. It was far too risky. An unseen landmine might be stepped on and ignite another explosion. His sales people were like many business teams who play it safe, silently colluding and hoping through divine intervention that Steve would change and become the leader that they all desired and deserved. In my mind, they were as cowardly as Steve.

Meanwhile, with his revenue stream gargling Listerine, tossing life preservers, and extracting emotional shrapnel from the Monday morning assault, Steve blundered on. Fear and insecurity triggered his behavior. He did not enter the world with those traits. Steve ignored his birthright authenticity, and instead, chose a conditioned and learned response that separated him from his true self. His behavior had nothing to do with a higher purpose, good intention, or any noble pursuit. He operated at his lowest and most unproductive level. Slowly but constantly, he was extinguishing the flame that he so desperately wanted to protect.

Steve's inability to manage appropriately his emotions of fear, anger, and anxiety, was his eventual downfall. Blowing up and venting steam may have been cathartic to him, but the rest of his team was scampering off to emergency wards. He was oblivious and closed to any constructive feedback that I had to offer. Fear will do that to a person. Denial and self-righteousness ruled. Others noticed. The owner eventually sold the company, and the new buyer immediately dismissed Steve and his destructive leadership style.

French philosopher Pierre Teilhard de Chardin perhaps said it best: "We are not human beings having a spiritual experience, we are spiritual beings having a human experience." Unfortunately, Steve allowed his human experience to dominate and block access to his spiritual, authentic self. The leader that Steve could have been was already inside of him. He had allowed his frightened ego to hold his authenticity hostage.

From the Zen tradition comes a story about a sculptor who had chiseled an incredible, anatomically perfect statue of an elephant out of an ancient and ugly granite rock. One day an admirer asked the artist, "How did you create such a beautiful animal out of that old and misshapen rock?" The sculptor replied humbly, "I simply chipped away all of the stone that was not the elephant." Take it off. Take it all off! It is all inside of you and you need to let it shine.

I am not suggesting that you become a postmodern, new millennium messiah walking through the plant and cubicles in a white robe hugging and distributing flower petals to your employees. The "group grope" leadership style has shortcomings as it decelerates decision making, involves too many people, and handcuffs leaders. I am not asking you to toss a bunch of feathered pillows around people when wanting to get something accomplished or to deliver a difficult message. What I am asking you to examine is this: Are your actions and behaviors furthering the individual, group, or organization in a positive and constructive manner? If what you are doing is only going to benefit yourself, paralyze your employees, and stall momentum, then immediately hit the reverse gear and reconsider. You do have a choice in this matter if you stay awake. Being awake is good.

Determine how your message will be best heard. You do not need to be perfect. Striving for perfection is futile and neurotic work. Give it up. I am advocating that you be appropriate. If what you are doing is not working, back up, and do something different. Pay attention. What you do and say does affect people's lives and your bottom line.

Through self-awareness and intention, effective leaders are able to sort and select their impulses according to what they are encountering. They have the ability to delay gratification and place inappropriate responses on hold. It is the right thing to do. Your people will appreciate it and respond in a positive manner.

## Individualize and give permission for others to do the same.

Business leaders come in a variety of packages. It is a Heinz 57. There is no defined formula in assembling the perfect chief. The business leader tribe is a multifaceted, differentiated, individualistic assortment of talents and characteristics. One thing I have noticed working with thousands of business leaders is that the blatantly successful ones are truly individualized, self-actualized human beings and are able to convey their individuality with a positive spin to the people whom they influence, inspire, and transform.

When I walked the corridors of my most successful clients' companies, I did not find an overabundance of "yes people." There were not many conformists strolling along-side humming some familiar tune of universal corporate compliance. Missing were a multitude of phonies, impostors, and charlatans in these flourishing businesses. These executives did not have sophisticated marketing departments creating their images and branding their personal identities. They were on their own, naked as the eyes of a clown, willing to stand in the organizational spotlight, warts and all. When the blemishes got in the way, they removed or censored them instead of insisting stubbornly to ignore or cover up what was producing negative outcomes.

Steve, the former branch manager, was not a part of this elite group. He was participating with the other folks. Granted, the winners occasionally lost their tempers, did not always do everything just right, say the right thing at the right moment, but people understood their humanity, and above all, trusted their intentions. Intention is everything.

I had the privilege of working with Jeff. He was a member of a CEO group that I facilitated in Seattle for fifteen years. He made an attempt at college but was too impatient to go through four years of formal education before marking his score in corporate life. This young entrepreneur danced and sang to a different tune. At age 20, he married his high school sweetheart, took a whack at corporate America, did well, but did not fit.

With borrowed funds, exhausted savings, and a friend for a partner, he launched his first company. At first, the ascent up his bell shaped curve was bumpy as he and his partner spent most of their time on the road, building distribution channels, relationships, and customers. They were away from their families and familiar surroundings. It was a road much traveled.

There were occasions when payroll was financed with personal credit cards, payables stretched, and receivables accelerated, but he stayed the course and eventually built a sizable net worth by growing the business, taking risks, and investing wisely. Eventually, he was living on the lake, luxury yacht docked out front, and enjoying the good life.

Jeff was an absolute original. What one saw at work, at the country club, at church, one witnessed at home with his family. He consistently wore the same face. The way Jeff was with his CEO peers was exactly how he was in all other situations. I always knew what to expect with Jeff, and so did the people who worked for him. Jeff was without fail what he claimed to be and his behavior constantly reinforced and claimed his identity. He was predictably generous, entrepreneurial, available, fun loving, shrewd, and willing to take risks. Being fired by Jeff was a ticket to a sizable severance package. If you needed a loan, he was available, financing for a new house, no problem. He took care of his family, employees, and friends without asking anything in return. He was so good and gracious to others that occasionally when he was inappropriate, it was quickly forgiven and forgotten.

One day, I was facilitating a planning session for him and his management team. I had allowed the group to slide off into an unproductive discussion regarding mission statements. They began arguing about whether a certain word meant this or meant that, if what they provided the customer was on purpose, mission, or vision? Should the right word be "dedicated" or "committed?" Does this sound familiar?

Their leader was becoming more irritated as the conversation drifted into what he termed "silliness." In retrospect, I agree. It had and I had allowed it to happen. Finally, after about twenty minutes of silliness, Jeff stood up, obviously upset, and proclaimed the meeting over. Finished! Done! He ordered his management team to stop wasting his and their time. Slamming his annual budget on the table, he suggested in no uncertain terms that his direct reports should get out of the conference room, go out and sell something, count inventory, order supplies, empty their waste paper baskets, do anything instead of continuing to do what they were doing.

"Let's not let this happen again." His words were not entirely unlike the message that Steve delivered consistently. How it was intended, delivered, received, and perceived was the difference.

Fortunately, Jeff had made enough positive deposits (Steve Covey-like) into his team that people could hear and respect what he was saying. They understood that he was right, that his intention was purely developmental and not punitive. Steve, on the other hand, had made so many destructive withdrawals from his sales force that the account was chronically overdrawn and the damage permanent. His message was heard with a tarnished mindset and filter.

Jeff demonstrated his humanness. He was not perfect. He was saying to his management team that it is okay to blow it once in awhile. Not all the time, but nobody in his organization was issued their walking papers for making the occasional mistake. To Jeff, mistakes are simply "mis-takes." When a "mis-take" occurs in filming a movie production, the director simply asks the actor to do it over and learn from the previous attempt. Jeff conveyed to all of us in that meeting that we were not mistakes; we were simply making one.

Jeff said to his managers that it is safe to bring all of yourself into this building. You do not have to check parts of yourself at the door unless your objective is to selfishly satisfy yourself and not the overall organization. Bring it on, but you had better learn! People are shown to the exit door for not learning. They learned and so did he.

Jeff was acknowledged in the CEO group that I was working with as the Godfather. Members respected him and sought his advice on personal and professional matters. He wore this hat well. His status was justified while he consistently extended himself to all others. Over the years, CEOs came and went in this particular group, but Jeff provided consistent stability and continuity. He represented everything that was gracious and effective in this unique gathering of successful and authentic business leaders.

After fifteen years, I stopped facilitating that group in February 2002 to satisfy my writing hunger and to expand my speaking career. It was time for a change and I had enjoyed a long and great run. During the last meeting with my clients, I conducted a closing ceremony where I publicly told each of the fifteen leaders how and what they had contributed to my life. I knew them intimately. I spoke from my heart and personalized my comments. Other hearts around the table opened as I offered my truth and experience with and about each member. When I concluded the exercise, Larry, president of a regional public bank, insisted that we reverse the process and have each member speak of my contribution to his or her lives. I half-heartedly protested but it was wonderfully rewarding as I listened to each member tell me what I had meant to each of them over the years. I had no idea. I could have gone several more laps around that table. It was my twelve minutes of fame, and I did not want it to end.

The Godfather was the last to speak. Jeff attempted to make eye contact with me but emerging and unanticipated tears blurred and diverted his vision. He struggled to speak but surging unfamiliar emotions idled his tongue and constricted his throat. While regaining his composure, he slowly and deliberately nodded his head toward me, his right hand clenched in a fist pointing skyward, his thumb up. He remained silent, as did all the others seated around that conference table, but everyone understood the message. Jeff's communication was flawless...how is yours?

It was an unintended and authentic moment that will remain in the group memory for a lifetime. Jeff, the anointed Godfather, with his kimono wide open, revealed to his colleagues, who he really was and what he was actually feeling. He was truly present, in the moment, coming out from behind his eyes with no excuses, no apologies, and perhaps just slightly embarrassed. Jeff had everyone's attention because we understood that his intent was pristine, pure, authentic, and unanticipated.

The invitation is for you to take the risk. Step out. Reveal. It is well worth the risk and the journey is eventually rewarding. Others will follow.

## Keep your "story" current.

I grew up in an absolute destitute family. Dysfunctional does not quite capture the entire experience. I understand it is relative, but the manner in which this band of characters chose to experience life was absurd and unnecessary. It was a chapter in my life, seasoned with poverty, abuse, and accompanied with a hearty dose of fundamental daily survival. I was on the 50-yard line, chin in hand, witnessing in naive wonderment, severe alcoholism, emotional and physical violence, sheriff foreclosures, and bottom of the barrel self-esteem. That was the Carlson family as I experienced it. I now understand that everyone was doing the best that they could with their level of consciousness at that time. I did not have that awareness until just recently.

When I was nine years old, my eleven year-old sister and I were unexpectedly shipped off on a Greyhound bus from Bell Gardens, California to Tacoma, Washington to live with a variety of distant relatives. We traveled light with only the clothes we wore, five dollars in cash, a jar of peanut butter, a butter knife, and a loaf of white bread. Timetables were a bit vague. They always were. That proposed schedule may have troubled others, but to us it seemed routine and quite normal. Mysteriously, our parents remained huddled in a slum trailer park in East Los Angeles plotting their next move to escape the bill collectors, encroaching neighborhood crime, and a worsening degradation of their desperate lives.

Somewhere between Fresno and Mt. Shasta, California, I decided that my family was untrustworthy and that I needed to take sole control of my life. If anyone was going to take care of Ole, it was going to be me. It was a heady and intoxicating decree for an innocent young boy not yet a decade on the planet. I concluded that independence and autonomy would be the strategies that would best serve me from that intersection forward. Those particular words were not a part of my childhood vocabulary, but I clearly understood the concepts and it seemed like the right and only available option that I had.

Behind an ivory-colored steering wheel, periodically slumped beneath a "Don't talk to the driver" public notice, veteran Greyhound bus driver, Mike, obediently and unconsciously steered our vehicle toward Puget Sound. Unbeknownst to him, in a window seat in the back row of his musty and nearly empty bus, a story was being formed that would be my north star for years to come. We are seldom aware that we are participating in someone's personal transformation.

As the Interstate 5 countryside passed by the dirty sliding glass bus window, I claimed accountability for creating my future. Subsequently, through the years, I earned my own money, chose my friends, lived where I wanted to live, went to schools that I selected, and did exactly what I wanted to do, when I wanted to do it, and how I wanted to do it. Nobody could tell this loner anything. Concepts of negotiation, intimacy, connection, community, feedback, family, and sharing were not on my radar screen. I was a great team player as long as I led the team. "Now everybody, huddle up and do it my way."

The strategy appeared to work as I broke free from the tyranny of the Carlson clan and created a life for myself that far exceeded anything that my immediate family had ever experienced or envisioned for them or for me. Evidence suggested that I was riding the right rail, headed in the right direction, doing the right things.

My benchmarks of success were obvious and plentiful. I became the only person in my immediate family to finish high school. I was awarded an academic/athletic scholarship to attend and graduate from the University of Washington. Fortune 500 companies employed and rewarded me with a six-figure income. I became a member of prestigious country clubs, socialized with high profile professionals, and lived in exclusive significant-income residential neighborhoods. Do not be misled. It was not always a straight-line climb. There were temporary setbacks. Unproductive luggage from the past unexpectedly tripped me. Fellow bus companion, sister Judy, had a similar ride, but that is another story. She is an inspiration and has her own tale to tell.

Unanticipated, the autonomous story surprisingly had numerous latent liabilities. Just when I thought all was permanent and would continue forever, here came the pratfall. I invited a psychologist to speak to my CEO group and conduct a personality profile on each member. I was tested along with the rest of the group. After completing and submitting the questionnaire, the psychologist later telephoned with the results.

"Congratulations for being number one," he began.

"In what category?" I asked.

"Having tested over 10,000 people, you scored number one in autonomy," he replied.

"Is that a good thing or a bad thing?" I wanted to know.

"It depends. How's it currently working?" he asked. I hate questions like that.

I proudly recited the first list regarding income, community status, Fortune 500 employers, education, and so forth.

He dug deeper and kept asking, "And what else?"

"Well, what do you mean 'what else'?" I answered impatiently.

"Ole, don't play confused and dumb with me. You know there's a 'what else'. There is more to the story than what you have shared with me. There's always more."

"Okay, I don't know how relevant this is or if it is any of your business, but here's some more," I said somewhat defiantly. "A couple of months ago, I completed my second marriage. It just wasn't working. Never did. I suppose I have a reputation for being arrogant, somewhat aloof, and at times, a lone wolf. That's what I hear from other people. I'm not so sure that I agree. You want more or is that enough of 'what else'?" I asked.

"Yes, if there is something else," he said.

"Well there is now that I think about it. I'm sort of estranged from my kids right now. We have drifted apart. It hurts. I spend most of my time flying around the world working with leaders I don't really know that well. When I'm home I'm basically alone most of the time in this condo that I live in."

"Is that what you want?" he asked.

"Not exactly, but sadly enough, it's what I have," I said hesitantly.

"Ole, what do you want?" he asked.

"For sure I want that first list to continue and I suppose I would like to reverse the 'what else' list and have just the opposite," I replied.

"No way unless you are willing to switch horses. The autonomy and independence ride is over and not going to get you to where you just told me you wanted to go. You're talking about a significant shift from your old familiar story of autonomy to a new tale of intimacy."

"Oh?" I replied.

Now that was a significant wake-up call. It was time to question whether my story was still effective and serving me well. Evidence was indicating clearly that what once provided for me at a very productive level was currently floundering on the rocks and showing signs of breaking apart. The autonomous, independent obsession was exhausted and worn. It was time to move on and create a new story that was more congruent with where I was in my life, but more important, where I desired and needed to go. It was time to get current. Conditions change, time passes, goals are reached, and what worked yesterday may be today's speed bump.

After considerable thought and deliberation, I made a different choice, one that is more timely and appropriate. Autonomy and independence were put out to pasture. It was time. Occasionally, curiosity interrupts their grazing to look up to see if I am making progress with my new story.

I am currently saddled upon the *intimacy* horse. It is what I really want now in my life. Giddy yap! It has been a long, and at times, an uncomfortable mount. I fall off frequently and find myself staring at the underbelly of this new graceful gelding. What a different perspective. Unfamiliar hoof marks sporadically appear on my anatomy. This is brand-new territory to consider and explore. At times, I long for my old story because it was such a valuable and familiar friend. It was my "Hi Ho Silver and Away" and I had it mastered. Alas, it had grown old and destined for the glue factory. When life becomes too familiar, comfortable, and predictable it is usually a sign that a change is in order.

Intimacy is now the compass setting. I have a new bride as my mentor, lots of embedded learning to draw upon, and an awakened awareness as my guiding shepherd. Daily, I see signs that the choice was appropriate and I am making progress.

Give it up if it is not working. I have heard hundreds of stories from leaders of businesses describing who they were. They were insightful and periodically accurate. Maybe, at one time, you needed to be a hard-nosed, driving SOB to accelerate you to your current destination. That story may have run its course. Check it out. Delegating and empowerment might be better and wiser choices. You make the decision. After all, it is your company. It is your net worth. You know the truth.

I was recently speaking to a CEO group in the Midwest. The facilitator asked a prospective new member to choose one word that best described him on the job. Don, the candidate, did not hesitate for a second and proudly announced to a room of new acquaintances, "I'm an asshole." A long silence followed his unanticipated blurt. Incoming! Something foul had been lobbed into the group's pristine crystal punchbowl.

The existing members quickly exchanged wide-eyed glances with one another as the air attempted to re-enter the room. I thought, "This is going to be interesting." It was! Don's self-assessment proved to be right on target as we experienced him throughout the rest of the session. He interrupted, argued, side talked, refused to turn off his cell phone, and took a disproportionate amount of airtime. The group elected to decline on his joining them and let him move on to a more suitable venue. Be careful how you depict yourself. You just might become what you claim to be.

Evaluate, calibrate, and trust the evidence suggesting that what you are doing needs adjusting or not. Let the feedback in and if it is overwhelmingly evident that a change is in order, do what needs to be done. Do not stubbornly fight back and hold your ground. This is not the time for righteous stands. What you are doing and how you are being, either is working or it is not. Where are you on your personal and professional journey? What is effective and what is not?

Bless your old story because it was a treasured comrade, that proved tremendously valuable in transporting you to your current destination. If no longer appropriate, put it to rest. A respectful eulogy is in order. With arms and heart wide open, welcome the newest version of you. You are simply accessing another part of yourself. It was there all along. There is no need for you to take a personal development course. You already have your ticket on a Greyhound bus bound to where you need and deserve to go.

For many years, I participated in marketing events to recruit CEOs for membership in the groups that I was facilitating and for others. A mass mailing was sent to CEOs with an invitation to attend a breakfast or lunch and learn about this valuable resource for business leaders. I would host these gatherings and in a 90-minute slot, tell the story and set the stage for enrollment into a peer group. What was astounding to me was that invitations would be sent to CEOs, and people with all their strengths and vulnerabilities kept showing up. Go figure!

Shakespeare said, "God has given us one face, yet we put on another." Resist the temptation. The more consistent and predictably authentic you are, the more you will influence your organization. You advertise for controllers, salespeople, administrators, and human beings keep coming to your door seeking employment and relationships. They crave to be led by other human beings whom they can trust, and you cannot accomplish that by insisting on being someone else. Wear that one original face well.

⌀═══╪═══⌀

**Review:** To be a successful and effective leader of a business you must:

1. Be who you are and not whom you think should be.

2. Bring your best self forward and change what is not working.

3. Individualize and give permission for others to do the same.

4. Keep your "story" current.

**Robust actions to take:**

1. What are some of your behaviors that get in your way of leading your business?


2. What prices are you paying for continuing those behaviors?


3. What is your story and is it still serving you well?

# 2

## STRATEGY TWO:
## Take Care of Yourself First—Then Others

*Don't compromise yourself.*
*You are all you've got.*
—Janice Joplin

∽

### Take the garbage out daily.

AS THE LEADER, IT IS 24/7. The demands on you are relentless. I suspect that you are not aware of the pressure and stress that you absorb on a daily basis while leading your organization. I have stood objectively in the wings and observed all that you do. From that perspective, it is overwhelming.

You hire and fire employees, negotiate loans, make sales calls, review financials, coach key reports, give reviews, facilitate meetings, confront poor performance, cut deals, sign contracts, have difficult conversations with customers, vendors, bankers, lawyers, and employees. That was all before lunch. Wait until the afternoon begins. These activities plus other factors that you bring from your home life can consciously or unconsciously contribute stress to your system.

Your stress bucket is becoming full and starting to overflow the rim. Beware. You are entering the stress-overload zone. Psychological and physiological demons are looming nearby.

Visualize a straightened metal paperclip bent back and forth, time and time again. What eventually happens? The paperclip snaps and breaks into two pieces. The question is what bend caused it to break? Answer: all of them as the accumulation of stress on the paperclip weakened it to the point of coming apart. You might encounter a similar experience with your version of being bent with persistent regularity. One day you might come apart brought on by a weakened and completely saturated system. Picture yourself out in front of your organization, bit in the mouth, running on empty, faced with leading a dynamic and demanding business. Not a pretty snapshot. Your version of the "snap" is making a poor decision, berating a key report, insomnia, drinking too much alcohol, overeating, avoiding important decisions, arguing with a loved one.

Do this. Journal your activities on any given business month and at the end of that period, review what you have logged. You will be flabbergasted with the volume of activities that you have chosen. Yes, I said chosen. We will talk about delegating in a following chapter.

If you accumulate stress on a daily basis then it seems reasonable to discover appropriate means to release it at the same frequency so that you can be net zero the following day. I have asked thousands of business leaders what they do to release stress and tension from their lives and, in return, I receive an alarming high percentage of blank stares and concerned looks. A former CEO client when asked this question replied, "I go home every night and get shit-faced. Does that count?" Not exactly. Stress reduction takes many forms. Whatever works for you is the right thing to do.

Strategies and activities that I have heard and that work for others are:

- ◆ "I run four miles everyday after work."

- ◆ "I listen to classical music before I go to bed."

- ◆ "I go home and dig in my garden."

- ◆ "I pray or meditate."

- ◆ "I sit down with my wife and we talk about our day."

- ◆ "I take a 20-minute nap midday."

- ◆ "I play the piano."

- ◆ "I just dumb down in front of the television."

- ◆ "I don't do squat."

That last one is frightening. Again, do whatever works, but please do something and do it often. Do not remain stationary, absorbing every punch straight on the chin and delude yourself that this strategy will suffice. It will not. You are a time bomb ticking away if you ignore this or play dumb. It is extremely difficult to effectively lead a business from a horizontal position in a local intensive care unit. Everyone in your outreach of influence deserves better, especially you.

The argument I often hear is that "I don't have the time to de-stress or shoehorn one more activity in my demanding calendar," or, "I can handle it." I am not buying that. It is not about time or the ability to deal with anything. It is about priorities and commitment. Be smart. You know you are. Some of you take better care of your import luxury automobile than you do your mind and body. When the red light comes on in your Mercedes, you promptly pull over and get assistance! Let us preempt and head off any impending disaster before your warning light suddenly appears on your computerized dash and you are between rest stops. You are not a replaceable parts machine.

Robert is the CEO of a $20 million manufacturing company. He is a consummate micromanager who insists on being in on everything that his company does. He is unreasonably driven and considers himself a real man who can deal effectively with anything that the world hands him. It is what he bilaterally decided is the truth about himself with the coaching and verification of his father. It is his story and he has stuck to it far too long.

Delegation, trust, and empowerment were foreign concepts to him. At least they all were until the day he snapped and was shackled by inertness. The fourteen-hour work days, the lack of sleep, eating a poor diet on the run, the stored anxiety, the interruptions in his day, and the lack of any release mechanism finally caught up with him. He ignored the signals that he was plummeting toward a black hole, got a severe case of target fixation, and bored himself and his company into a deep and forbidding crater. A mushroom cloud hovered over his personal and professional life.

Harvey Wiley, legendary New York boxing icon commented on fighting Ali, "Things just went sour gradually all at once. He'll pick you and peck you, peck you and pick you, until you don't know where you are." That is what happened to Robert. He ignored the constant "rat-a-tat-tat" on his internal well-being. Denial had become his mantra. Woody Woodpecker was embedded on his forehead pecking away at his financial, mental, emotional, and physical health. Justification was easy and familiar. The price he paid was difficult and unexpected.

Robert is now spending what used to be his equity-building time in therapy and rehabilitation clinics trying to comprehend how this all happened. He is learning how to delegate and ultimately reclaim his life. The company is on financial and emotional life support while he recovers. The mushroom cloud is slowly dissipating. Remember what doctors are taught in medical school: do no harm, especially to yourself. Get the picture?

## Satisfy your "what if."

I would wager that you have read somewhere or heard someone say that you should be a "servant leader," that the customer is "always right," that you should have an "open door" policy in your business, that the "buck stops here." Enough already! I understand the concepts, but I have observed many of you taking this to an unbearable extreme. You wind up with too much on your overcrowded plate, attempting to please an ever expanding and demanding internal and external community, leaving you with no time or energy for yourself.

Many of you do this because you truly believe that it is the right thing to do or it is all that you know. You might have a high need to be liked or you unilaterally concluded that you have no other choice. Perhaps a business role model or a parent led in this manner, maybe you avoid confrontation, and it is fearful for you to say "no" to employees, customers, vendors, and all the other people in your life. In the years working with business leaders, I believe that I have heard it all. Here is the deal. If you do not take care of yourself, *cheated and depleted* is potentially going to be engraved on your tombstone. At the end of the day, you are going to feel physically and emotionally exhausted and, on some conscious or unconscious level, ripped off.

My best friend lives in Spokane, Washington. I met Frank (his nickname is "Ginge") in 1963 as a freshman at the University of Washington. We were talented football players on full scholarships, competing for the same position, and living in rival fraternities. With that as our initial platform, we nurtured a friendship that has never wavered nor weakened over the past four decades. I absolutely have come to love this wonderfully devoted friend.

The week before my fiftieth birthday, I received a telephone call from Ginge. I assumed he was calling to wish me a happy birthday. He was not. He was calling from a prone position in a New York City hospital bed recovering from a ruptured colon, emergency surgery, and missing approximately 18 inches of some internal plumbing. He was groggy, considerably lighter, and had nearly died from the incident. The occasion was a wake-up call prompting him to reflect on how he wanted to live the second half of his life. One of the issues that he wanted to explore was our friendship. Ginge told me he wanted more face-to-face time with his best friend. He asked us to make a commitment to one another that from that day forward each year we would go somewhere and just hang. We could play golf, fish, eat great meals, reminisce about the past, preview one another's future. No kids, no spouses, and no other friends were to be invited. We did not have to seek permission from anyone. I agreed, and we have been going on our annual excursions ever since. You might see us in the future in some airport shuffling along with walkers, golf clubs, various tubes inserted here and there, and in fits of laughter.

I suspect some might view these getaways as self-serving. I did at first and now I have a different perspective. Yes, I agree the trips are expensive, the time is difficult to find, loved ones feel left out, and guilt sometimes enters the picture, but the return on investment is "MasterCard Priceless." The time I spend with Ginge keeps me mentally, spiritually, physically, and emotionally healthy. I am overflowing with laughter, fun, caring, thinking, and a few tears. I believe that I deserve and I am worthy of, at a minimum, one break per year.

Reward yourself. You are so accustomed to taking care of others that you often exclude yourself. Declare something just for you and act upon it with the same vigor and attention that you do when satisfying other people's needs. Buy that Harley and take motorcycle-driving lessons. Float the Colorado River with college friends. Have a night out on the town playing poker. Go shopping without reservation. Take a snooze in the middle of the day. Go to the gym at noon. Take piano lessons. Write the book. Do whatever makes you happy and fulfilled. Do it now. Is it not possible that if you do something for yourself others will benefit?

I fear that some of you may experience a "what if" conversation with yourself when it is too late to do anything about it. You know what I mean. "What if I had only?" Nobody wants or deserves to have that exchange with themselves or with their loved ones.

Terry was a CEO client in his midforties. He was self-made, rising from the trades and eventually creating a multimillion dollar business building custom homes for professionals in his community. He was not an educated, brilliant businessperson, but he was sound, honest, smart, a learner, and giving it all he had. I was proud to be professionally associated with him and call him my personal friend.

One morning Terry slipped out of bed, meandered into the bathroom to shave, looked into the mirror above the sinks, and stopped breathing. Staring back at him was an unfamiliar and concerned face. His skin was dark yellow as if during the night someone had snuck into his bedroom and painted him the color of a caution light. He called out for his wife, Barbara, to come and look. She did and then rushed to the telephone to call their family doctor to find out what was happening to her husband. Yellow is not good.

Terry was able to go in that morning to see the doctor because of their friendship (try that today in a metropolitan area). It was not good news; an afternoon exploratory surgery revealed pancreatic cancer ravaging his body in an advanced and unstoppable stage. He had perhaps three to four months on the planet and that was it. It was a devastating blow for everyone involved in Terry's life.

Over the next three months, Terry made every effort to attend the monthly CEO meetings that I facilitated. He was exhausted, losing weight, in considerable pain, and could only manage to be with his business colleagues for a few hours of the all-day meeting. The time he spent with us was invaluable in helping us reset what was important in our lives. Yes, we were businesspeople and owners of successful organizations, but we also had families, friends, hobbies, and lives to be lived fully with robust passion and self-initiated fulfillment. Terry was firm and relentless with his message. "Take care of all your life's business and do it now." It was a call to duty for everyone in the room. He had and deserved our attention.

On a Sunday morning approximately three months following Terry's fatal diagnosis, I received a call from Barbara requesting that I come immediately to their house. I knew what this meant and had been dreading this private invitation for weeks. Terry was not going to be with us much longer.

Upon arriving at their home, Barbara met me at the front door and we exchanged hugs. She pointed simply to the upstairs bedroom where Terry, in a hospice situation, was resting. She was worn and distant. This stalwart woman had absorbed a heavy toll and was doing all that she could to work through the many issues regarding Terry's eventual fate. She had remained strong and a focal point for friends, family, and business associates throughout the entire ordeal. There was no need to say anything. The communication was exquisite.

As I walked up the steps to the master bedroom, I began shaking and feeling more frightened than any other time in my life. I had never been in this situation before. Where was the script? I was certain that I would fall apart, say the inappropriate thing, or just lose it in front of a person who deserved so much more of me in this intimate moment. When I entered the room and encountered Terry for the first time in a couple of weeks, I gasped at how weak and small he had become. His Popeye forearms had been reduced to slender willows, his handsome face drawn and stretched taut across his cheekbones, his strong, powerful body now frail and a fraction of what it had been.

He noticed my discomfort and whispered in a feeble, hoarse, voice, "Ole, would you please come in. You are still on a retainer and I have some hours to cash in. Lie beside me so you can hear. I have a few things I want to say. It's getting late."

Terry began by thanking me for what I had contributed to his life, how I had helped him with the business, and how I had been a good and faithful friend. I became less fearful and more engaged in this most important conversation as I listened and remained attentively still lying next to him. It was a sacred moment that deserved my fullest attention.

"There is one more thing; it is a request," Terry continued, looking more fatigued than when I first came in, his voice becoming weaker, and his pace considerably slower. "I know that you speak to many of my business colleagues, people like me all over the world, and I have a message that I would like for you to pass on to them."

"Of course I will. Anything. What is it?" I replied.

In a seemingly sad voice Terry said, "Please tell them to never, never subordinate to their business anything that they believe is really important to them. Business is only one part of who we are. Ole, this thing is all-consuming. I think I knew it at the time but I just ignored what was happening. I never seemed to get to the stuff that was vital to my life and to my happiness. I mean, my family, health, hobbies, friendships, you know. Do you get what I'm saying?"

I nodded, hoping that he knew I understood and softly I asked the question that was begging to be asked, "What stuff didn't you get to, Terry? What didn't you pay attention to?"

Tears welling in his eyes, his voice becoming more faint, Terry replied, "I never took the time to be Geppetto."

"What?" I said, seeking clarification.

"I didn't stand shoulder to shoulder with Pinocchio, you know, with my son David, together crafting beautiful wood furniture with our hands. I had the tools and the skill. Geppetto taught Pinocchio how to be a little boy and eventually become a man. I never did that with David," Terry replied sternly.

"You did the best you could with your level of awareness at the time. Don't be so hard on yourself," I said.

"No, no. Let me finish. We could have spent wonderful time together, one on one. We could have been like the main characters in the movie the *Field of Dreams*, father and son, playing catch until dark with unspoken communication. It could have been our version. I could have left him with that experience and skill. He could have remembered me for that. Now it's too late. I can't even hold a tool let alone stand shoulder to shoulder with anyone. He doesn't really know me and I don't really know him the way I should have and wanted to."

"Have you told David what you just shared with me?" I asked.

Terry replied, "Yes, yesterday we spent some time together. I told him that I loved him deeply and that I did the best that I could. He said he understood. It was hard and I'm not sure he got it."

Terry had just told me his "what if." He was current with David. My guess is that David did get it and will always remember his dad the way Terry wanted. My friend and client passed away shortly after that conversation, embraced and comforted by his family and friends. Most of his fellow CEO colleagues attended the memorial and were there to say farewell to our fallen comrade. We had lost a member of our tribe. Some could not handle it and stayed away. Terry would have understood.

For the next twelve months, the CEO group kept a conference table place setting for Terry along with his name tent at our monthly meeting to honor him and to remind all of us to live a more balanced and more fulfilling life, and to make sure that our priorities were in proper order. People come and go in our lives, and when they go, they leave the best of themselves behind with us. Terry certainly did.

Pay attention. One day one of you may go to the mirror to shave or put on makeup and your mortality may be staring back at you suggesting that there is little time left to do the things that are really important. Like the saying goes, in the last moments, none of us wants our tombstones to say that we wished we had spent more time at the office.

Thank you, Terry, for this reminder. God bless you and safe journey, old friend.

## Strive for appropriate balance.

I believe firmly that you can stay in the fast lane for a significant amount of time if you create a high degree of balance in your life. You are more than a leader of a successful business. The problem is that most of you identify with only one facet of yourself, the businessperson. "I am a businessperson," you declare unconsciously, limiting many other possibilities in your life. You are much more. You are a spouse, parent, athlete, and you have many other dimensions of yourself to explore and expand.

Keep in mind that you are a holistic spiritual being who on occasion runs a prospering business. What if you approached all of the nonbusiness areas of your life with the same vigor, enthusiasm, and attention that you do when working with the business? What would your life be like? Be honest. What are you doing about you relationships, your finances, your health, your spiritual life, your personal interests, your family and all those other facets of your existence that comprise your total life? Periodically we need to reset these areas. Habits, staleness, and familiarity can set in and dull our experience. Many of you spend the majority of your time and energy on the business, but at what cost? I do not blame you. I am not here to pass judgment. I would probably do the same thing if it were not for all the observations and knowledge I have accumulated in the past seventeen years working with you in the trenches. You have been extraordinary teachers.

Here is the deal. If you had more balance in your life, I believe you could perform at a much higher level in your business. In addition, if your business improves, you have more time and resources to broaden your experience of life and around and around it goes. It does not have to be a paradox or one or the other. Ease into it by starting to dilute and focus your business activities and see yourself in a more holistic way. You do not have to dive into the deep end. Wade out from the shallows, one step at a time.

I have never encountered a population of people who are better at creating tangible results (money or what money can buy) than yours. You have figured out this one. You live in a world of abundance, and it is perfectly acceptable to cast the net and haul in the catch. You deserve as much of it as you can acquire constructively. An issue with you is: when is enough, enough and when does this get out of balance with the intangible (values, purpose, behaviors, spiritual) side of your life?

Your competitive nature gets in the way. You build up a net worth of $X and you find out that a competitor, country club member, or colleague has $Y and off you go, bit in mouth, lathered up, streaking to the lead. This can be healthy if what you are doing to create the tangible success also brings you fulfillment and allows you time and energy to participate in other aspects of your life. Without that fulfillment or variety, you can run out of gas, having plenty of toys in your inventory, but nobody to play with. Remember: he who dies with the most toys still dies and somebody else gets the toys or winds up squabbling over them after the funeral.

My wife, Sue Ann, and I live in a vast golf complex, with multiple courses, clubhouses, and workout facilities in Southern California. During our first month in our new home, we were excited about playing all of the courses and meeting the existing members. One day we scheduled a tee time at one of the links that we had not played previously. It was early in the morning and a postcard perfect golf day. As we drove up to the first tee box in our new golf cart, the starter came over, welcomed the two of us, and asked if we would be willing to play in a threesome with one of the members of the club who was looking for a game.

"Terrific, you bet!" I replied. "I'd welcome the chance to meet someone new who is familiar with the course that we're playing. A win-win for all of us."

The starter introduced Sue Ann and me to the veteran member. He shook our hands and handed me his business card. I thought that was unusual but, wanting to be courteous, I took the card, and was surprised to see a color picture of this club member standing beside a Lear Jet. I concluded that he must be in the aviation business, but turning the card over, I discovered that he owned a company that manufactured bearings for heavy equipment.

It was impossible not to notice that his golf cart was different from the "vanilla" cart we owned. His was a candy-apple red, custom built, miniature Jaguar with a CD deck, an overhead cooling system, a hands-free telephone, and dark leather seats. Harnessed on the back of his golf cart was the largest and most expensive golf bag and set of state-of-the-art clubs that I have ever seen. To top it off, our new playing partner was dressed exquisitely head-to-toe in the latest golf attire.

As we approached the tee box on number one he asked, "Ole, would you like to make this interesting, have some fun?"

"Uh, sure." I replied. "What do you have in mind?"

"How about a buck a hole, and a five dollar bonus for lowest overall net," he answered. "Let's keep it simple."

"You're on." The competitive monster in me reared up and replied, "Woman, into the cart. The game is on." After determining the handicap bookkeeping and adjusting, off we went with our newfound playing companion.

We were playing even until I got on a hot streak and started to win successive holes on the back nine. He was becoming more irritated as I teed off first, three consecutive times. We were standing at the number thirteen tee box, a par five with a blind first shot over a hill. I asked, "Any trouble over the hill?"

"Nope, no trouble," he offered while quietly reaching for an iron in his oversized golf bag. "Blast away!"

I did and when I drove my cart over the hill for my second shot, I discovered the lake. No ball in sight and not even a ripple was present where the golf ball had entered the water. No trouble for him as he hit a five iron off the tee to the crest of the hill and was bone dry for his second shot.

He recorded a five on his card and I penciled in a double bogey. After a slow burn on the next tee box, I challenged him on his advice and he replied brusquely, "We are playing for money. This is a competition and you should have done your homework. It's your responsibility to know what you're getting into. There would have been no trouble had you selected the proper club."

I was astonished and settled on the spot. "Have a nice day," I said as Sue Ann and I drove back to the clubhouse.

Maybe he was a bit too focused on the tangible side of his life. Maybe he was slightly out of balance. Maybe he did not know any better. Maybe he was just a jerk. In any event, one can still find him at the number one tee box on all the courses with one bag on the back of his golf cart looking for a game.

## Stretch and go beyond comfort.

Michelangelo said, "The greatest danger for most of us is not that our aim it is too high and we miss it, but that it is too low and we reach it." Most of you have only a limited view of what you can actually accomplish. I suspect that you are using only a small percentage of your potential. Do not get me wrong. You have achieved at a level that few can only imagine or, perhaps, more accurately, cannot imagine. The question is: what is getting in your way to access more of your potential in both your personal and professional life? We can all conjure up our own reasons and excuses. Here are a few I have heard:

- ◆ "This is all I want out of life."

- ◆ "I got tired."

- ◆ "I didn't know that those other parts of me existed."

- ◆ "I've done better than most people."

- ◆ "I settled into a comfort zone."

- ◆ "I ran out of money, time, and energy."

- ◆ "I don't deserve more."

- ◆ "I'm an imposter."

- ◆ "I just lucked out."

- ◆ "I don't know how to take my life to the next level."

All are valid explanations and your reality is truly your reality. You own it. I respect that. Maybe the more valid answer lies in the fact that what you did to become successful in business never transferred to your personal life. You never became aware of the process so you could deliberately replicate it and teach others. I am attempting to widen your life's band and have you experience yourself at an expanded and balanced level. You deserve it.

Following are the steps I would wager that you are taking to be a successful businessperson, and I guarantee you they will work equally well in your personal life.

**Step One:** You have great clarity about what you want to achieve in your life. (Low performance people use confusion as a strategy for staying stuck.)

**Step Two:** You have the ability to sense the future and move toward your fresh pictures, thoughts, and emotions. (Low performance people focus on the past, allowing outdated pictures, thoughts, and emotions to determine their future.)

**Step Three:** Your inner dialogue is positive about yourself and about life in general. (Low performance people have a negative inner dialogue about themselves and life.)

**Step Four:** Your emotions are positive regarding your future and yourself. (Low performance people's emotions are negative.)

**Step Five:** You embrace a high degree of accountability and self-efficacy. (Low performance people embrace a high degree of subordination and helplessness.)

**Step Six:** You are real about your life. (Low performance people are in denial and fantasy.)

**Step Seven:** You work diligently and with intelligence. You pay the price through sacrifice, delaying gratification, and doing whatever it takes morally to get the job done. (Low performance people believe the world owes them comfort and success.)

Martin is in his early sixties. He is a member of a CEO group in California that I had spoken to about seven years ago. The material that I covered with the group dealt with creating balance and implementing the seven steps.

Martin had figured out how to be relatively successful in business. He had achieved financial security for himself and his family but had reached a plateau. The rest of his life was, by his judgment, mediocre at best. He was not in the finest of health. He had limited energy. His relationship with his wife over the years was becoming stale. He did not have many close friends, and life was becoming dull and predictable. Conversations with others were becoming redundant with little new ground being explored. His enthusiasm for life was seemingly waning. He had not tried anything new in his life for a decade and was beginning to agree with Peggy Lee as he wondered, "Is this all there is?"

Recently I returned to talk to this group at a retreat with their spouses and perhaps reacquaint myself with Martin. My material was essentially the same as before except for a few new stories and a slightly different emphasis. I was surprised to find that Martin was still a member of the group and evidently had broken through the doldrums of seven years ago. He looked great, energized, and healthy. Just before one of the breaks in the seminar, Martin raised his hand and asked if he could share something important with the rest of the group. Curious as to what he had in mind, I said fine.

"I'm not here to promote Ole Carlson, but I have to tell you this guy that we have in front of us literally saved my life," Martin began.

"Ah come on Martin," I protested. "But please do continue for as long as you'd like."

"When Ole first spoke to this group some time ago, I was in the tank. You guys remember that? Well, I am here to tell you that this stuff works. It's not magical, mystical, or rabble babble psycho bullshit. Simply stated, life can work for us if we put this material to use. When I did it, most everything in my life changed for the better and I have never felt more positive about myself or about what I have accomplished. That's the damn truth! I am a living, breathing, testimonial turnaround and it was all because I did what Ole is suggesting."

We seldom are aware of when we are facilitating someone's personal and professional transformation. Evidently, Martin concluded that there was a lot more to life and that he had only scratched the surface of what could be possible for him. Martin spoke with conviction, renewed energy, and enthusiasm. His wife beamed while he talked about their re-energized relationship. He spoke passionately about the growth and profitability in his business, about taking it to another level by bringing in new talent and changing his micromanager ways. He had reacquainted himself with dusty and seemingly worn-out friends and had brought new people into his life. He was working out at the gym and physically feeling better than at any other time that he could recall. His spiritual life was rejuvenated and more in congruence with his current station in life. He had done all of this by himself, armed with only the seven basics steps of creating a rewarding and fulfilling reality. That was all he really need-ed. I believe firmly that deep down inside we know what to do. Get the ball rolling and get out of the way.

Here comes the preacher. Do not settle. You are much more than what you are experiencing. Take it to the limit. You are special because you are in the chair of the leader of a successful business. As a percentage of the population, not many people have accomplished what you have done. Digest, accept, and give yourself credit. If it feels right, if you believe it is right for you, take it up a notch in all areas of your life. Your business will benefit as you expand and widen your experience of this unique entity called you.

**Review:** To be a successful and effective leader of a business you must:

1. Take the garbage out daily.
2. Satisfy your "what if."
3. Strive for appropriate balance.
4. Stretch and go beyond comfort.

**Robust actions to take:**

1. For one work month, journal all of the activities that you are involved in on a daily basis. Please include everything whether it seems stressful or not. Rate each activity on a scale of one to five with one being the least stressful and five being the most stressful. Pay special attention to the fives. Identify what you are doing on a daily basis to relieve the stress, and if there is not any activity, choose

one that allows you to drain the accumulated tension from your system.

2. Record what you have done for yourself in the past six months that was just for you. If the list is short or nonexistent, decide right now to declare something in the immediate future. Approach this activity as if it really mattered and with the same robust passion and interest that you do when taking care of others. This is a non-negotiable contract with you. Make a commitment to honor it no matter what.

3. Declare one goal in each of the following categories that you will achieve in the next twelve months.

### Financial:

My goal is to…

My obstacle is…

My robust first step is to…

### Spiritual:

My goal is to…

My obstacle is…

My robust first step is to…

### Personal:

My goal is to…

My obstacle is…

My robust first step is to…

**Health:**

My goal is to...

My obstacle is...

My robust first step is to...

**Relationships**

My goal is to...

My obstacle is...

My robust first step is to...

4. Identify and commit to unreasonably reset yourself in all areas of your life. Examine where you have fallen asleep and give yourself a wake-up call. You deserve it, the people in your life deserve it, and I guarantee that once you become fully awake again your life will dramatically change for the better.

# 3

## STRATEGY THREE:
## Lead the Organization—Let Others Manage It

---

*A leader should not get too far in front of*
*his troops or he will be shot in the ass.*
—JOSEPH CLARK

∽

### Own the leadership role.

IF YOUR NAME IS IN THE TOP SLOT on the organization chart, you are it. It does not matter how you arrived there, what package you come in—male or female, tall or short, young or old, obese or thin, articulate or tongue-tied, experienced or an unsure rookie, your job as the leader in your organization is to:

♦ Inspire, influence, and transform your people.

♦ Set the corporate compass with your vision.

♦ Be decisive.

♦ Drive the business with your principles.

♦ Delegate, and get busy doing what you are paid to do.

I have the honor of working worldwide with thousands of successful leaders of all business types and sizes. This is what I am learning about them: they have the ability to attract and lead talented followers. When they turn around, they see a column forming behind them of mostly familiar faces and occasionally some strangers attempting to crowd in the queue. If there is no column behind you, you are simply on a lonely walk.

Effective leaders are able to communicate explicitly to the organization where they want to go and to motivate their direct report managers to get them to that destination and far beyond. Rosalynn Carter suggests, "A leader takes people where they want to go. A great leader takes people where they don't necessarily want to go, but ought to be." I believe this is what effective leadership is all about. The short list above represents a proven road map to high achievement and can be your formula for continued success in your business.

Let us keep it simple so you do not become overwhelmed and bogged down trying to sort through what you are expected to do. There is an abundance of material telling you how to become a better leader. Most of it is sound, expert advice. It is not as if we are in a vacuum of information regarding the subject. Investigate what is out there. Select what works for you, and above all else, follow the proven advice and methods of your peers who appreciate and understand what it is like to be in your shoes. You can trust this tribe like no other. It is a credible bunch.

**Inspire, influence, and transform your people.**

You are the only person in your company who has the right to infiltrate the organization chart at all levels and cross all functional boundaries with no limitations and no border guards. Understand that you cannot do that sitting in your soft leather swivel chair behind a closed door pouring over a spreadsheet or reading the *Wall Street Journal*. Get to know your people. The carpet to and from your employees should be frayed and worn.

When I was a freshman pledge in the Phi Delta Theta fraternity at the University of Washington, the upperclassmen insisted that all the new pledges get to know the other 110 brothers in the fraternity house. There were fines and spats if you did not know their names, where they were from, and what they were studying. Same thing applies here. Make yourself visible and leverage the fact that you have an almost godlike impact on the people who work for you. Okay, maybe deity status is an overstatement of the truth. However, at the very least, you have parental rank and that is good enough to make a significant difference in someone's life. One good word from you goes a long way, and as I have said, because I believe that this is important, we never know when we are facilitating another person's transformation.

David Whyte, the English author and poet, was the featured keynote speaker at a CEO facilitators' conference in Southern California that I attended in 1999. He held the audience spellbound as he wove together sound business principles with his original poetry and stories. He left the spectators with a new language and a fresh, new way to view their role with their CEO clients.

The conference leaders believed that David and I comple-
mented one another and would make a good team. We
agreed, and I designed a three-day personal transformation
workshop that highlighted David for one of the three days.
Our venue was the perennial five-star Broadmoor Resort and
Spa in Colorado Springs, Colorado. Not bad. Our partici-
pants were business executives and professional facilitators.
It was a magical three days in a wondrous Rocky Mountain
setting. Does it get any better than that?

David shared with the group a poem he had written that
captures what people, who happen to be employees, want, and
desire, in this fast-moving, postmodern business environment.

### LOAVES AND FISHES
#### —DAVID WHYTE

*This is not*
*the age of information.*
*This is not*
*the age of information.*
*Forget the news,*
*and the radio,*
*and the blurred screen.*
*This is the time*
*of loaves and fishes.*
*People are hungry,*
*and one good word is bread*
*for a thousand.*

—from *The House of Belonging*

I noticed that one of my clients never complimented or
verbally rewarded his employees. When I challenged him on

his behavior he replied, "I'll be damned if I'll ever say something good to any of them about them because my dad never said anything good to me about me." How is that for logic? Eventually I found him to be trainable and have encouraged him to enroll in a twelve-step recovery program designed to help him get over it and if for nothing else, pass on a few "atta persons" for business reasons. This is low hanging fruit that does not cost a penny and has an infinite return. Leadership expert John Maxwell said, "A big man is one who makes us feel bigger when we are with him." Invest!

Albert Einstein said, "Only a life lived for others is worth living." Admittedly, Albert was one of the sharpest knives in the 20th Century drawer and I respect his opinion. However, I would like to rein that in just a hair. I believe Albert's stance in life can be taken to an unproductive extreme (see Chapter Two).

I struggle with stretching the servant leader model to the outermost exhausting boundaries. Be reasonable with yourself. Identify and focus on the top 20 percent of your people and devote 80 percent of your time and resources furthering them along. The bottom feeders might get the joke and some of them could possibly rise above where they are currently resting and hiding (and they are resting and hiding, do not kid yourself). Do not spend your valuable time trying to elevate those floundering around and stuck ankle deep in foul-smelling corporate sediment. Stay with your winners and demonstrate to them how to get to where you currently are and to where you are headed in the future. That is being a leader.

In my former work with CEOs, I would meet for two hours once a month with each one of the clients. That was

sixteen appointments every month come rain or shine, sick-
ness, or conflicting tee times. It was an essential and
differentiating element of the process. My clients and I
referred to the meetings as one-to-ones. The sessions were
scheduled, closed-door, confidential, and at times very
intense get-togethers.

The client and I explored what he or she was working on,
whether they were stuck, where they were going, and all
other topics that mattered in their personal and professional
lives and wanted to avoid discussing. We sparred back and
forth from a prepared agenda, and at the conclusion of the
meeting, the CEO committed to certain actions that would
accelerate him/her forward toward implementation. High
level listening, relentless clarifying, and resisting offering
sage advice were the main skills that were demanded of me.
I learned how to listen objectively without judgment or
blame. Try that. It is not as easy a task as it may seem. Some
of the conversations frightened the highly paid consultant
out of me and I wanted to scream out with veins popping on
my forehead, "Are you out of your ever-loving mind?"
Nevertheless, I remained poker-faced, heart pounding and
kept exploring. When appropriate, I held their feet to the fire
and introduced them to the concept of accountability, which
I hoped had a high degree of transference to their leadership
relationship with their managers.

Many of my most successful leaders replicated the one-to-
one exercise with their corporate keepers. The one-to-one
process with their managers allowed them to develop their
top 20 percent, and to spend quality, uninterrupted time with
the people who were responsible for increasing their net

worth and overall compensation. I wholeheartedly recommend that you do the same. You need more face-to-face time with your perennial winners.

Rising stars want to learn and grow. It is their hunger and they are voracious consumers. American social philosopher, Eric Hoffer states, "In the times of rapid change, learners inherit the Earth, while the learned find themselves beautifully equipped to deal with a world that no longer exists." Do not tell me you do not have the time or they would not be interested. You do and they are! Keep in mind that the more they increase their personal inventory of skills, knowledge, and experience, the more valuable they become in a free agent business environment to you and to others (more on that later). It is the "others" that should be of most concern to you. Top people understand and are eager to implement this personal advancement strategy. I do not blame them. Stay engaged. Lassoing talented people is an ongoing challenge. Other interested people with resources equal to or exceeding yours are talking with them over expense account dinners and extra dry, two-olive martinis, offering them opportunities that they may find difficult to refuse.

Aggressive recruiters are actively pursuing industry stars. I was speaking at a banking conference about the free agent situation when someone in the audience raised his hand in utter frustration and bellowed, "I'm damn sick and tired of these blasted flesh peddlers calling into my organization hustling my top people." Before I could respond someone else in the audience cried out, "You should be more concerned when they stop calling!" Good point.

It seems to be a classic Catch 22. You are investing your money, time, experience, and wisdom in developing your key people, and one day, off they go to start their own businesses, perhaps even competing directly against you. Consider this: they could be your successor and an integral and only participant in your exit strategy. They might become a valuable customer or have some other future strategic relationship or alliance with you and your company. While you have them, they may accelerate your company to heights you never considered or had the ability to accomplish. Enjoy them while you can. They are very much like you.

Growing your winners is a sound business investment. When it is all said and done, you will know that you were instrumental in assisting another person in reaching out to live the quality of life that you created for yourself. Down deep, that is what you want. It is a form of paying it forward. You will sleep well at night having accomplished that.

Use the one-to-one to *inspire* your top performers to go far beyond where they currently reside. Assist them in creating a vivid picture of their future selves. Eleanor Roosevelt said, "The future belongs to those who believe in the beauty of their dreams." Help your key people define and realize their dreams.

When I was 14 years old, Sid Parker, a just-out-of-college high school math teacher and baseball coach, voluntarily took me under his wing and assisted me in constructing a picture of my future self that was well beyond what I could have ever imagined. Periodically on a Saturday, Sid would drive us the 90 miles from Oak Harbor to Seattle and we would explore the University of Washington campus, Greek

Row, the library, the football stadium. His message was consistent. "Ole, you can attend this university, live in those fraternity houses, study in that library, and play in that stadium. Forget your past, it is all possible." It all came true because of the picture he helped me construct for myself.

Share your journey with your talent. You are already there or nearly there. Show them the steps that you took, the speed bumps that you glided or bumped over, what to leverage, and what to discard. Do not assume that they know, because if they did they would be in a seat similar to yours having this talk with their direct reports. Engage in a continuous conversation relative to their career path. Explore areas that they need to develop, skills they need to acquire, behaviors that would benefit them as they move forward in their careers. Provide them opportunities to stretch beyond immediate comfort, make resources available for them, and above all, remain in active conversation.

We *influence* others through coaching, mentoring, and role modeling. Coaches teach, demonstrate techniques, challenge, and hold people accountable. Mentors mostly instruct and pass on to the student what they have learned by experience and what they know works. Role models set the example by their presence, activities, and being visible.

The most important person to anyone in the workplace is his or her immediate boss. Leverage this position. According to our relativity friend Albert Einstein, "setting an example is not the main means of influencing another, it is the only means." You do not always have to be perfect but you had better understand that you are being watched and interpreted by your people day by day, hour by hour, minute by minute, second by second. You are in the corporate fishbowl, magnified completely out of proportion. Be aware and beware.

Show your employees what success looks, tastes, sounds, and feels like. Nudge them along and allow them to make their own mistakes (within reason) and to learn from their own experiences. Help them raise the bar on their performance by spending shoulder-to-shoulder time (Geppetto-like) with them and passing on to them what you have learned.

Business expert Kenneth Blanchard believes, "The key to successful leadership today is influence, not authority." Influence does not mean control. Once you intentionally control another person, you no longer influence at any significant level. Agree upon the objectives, set clear expectations, and get out of the way. Learn to step in only when appropriate. Let go of your need to immediately rescue.

Conrad Hilton suggests, "Success seems to be connected with action. Successful people keep moving. They make mistakes, but they don't quit." Your duty is to keep the keepers moving along on their journey and refusing to let them quit. As Confucius said, "I hear and forget. I see and remember. I do and I understand."

We have in the one-to-one a perfect venue for facilitating *transformation*. We can make dreams visible for our employees who are temporarily asleep or blinded by repetitious, too familiar, and comfortable tasks. Mahatma Ghandi reminds us, "A friend is someone who knows the song in your heart and can sing it back to you when you have forgotten the words." Look at every interchange with your key people as an opportunity to move them beyond where they currently stand or are stuck. Peter Drucker states, "Leadership is not magnetic personality—that can just as well be a glib tongue. It is not making friends and influencing people-that is flattery. Leadership is lifting a person's vision to high sights, the raising of a person's performance to a higher standard, the building of a personality beyond its normal limitations."

Conversations with your managers should be more than just an exchange of meaningless clichés or a habitual and mindless slapping of high fives. Sing the songs back to your stars. Challenge them to get involved with their own personal and professional evolution. Ultimately, these encounters should conclude with you having learned something new, and your employees having received a challenging assignment, as well as feedback that will propel them forward or correct ineffective behavior. And, above all, they should leave wanting to come back for more. Be intentional with your conversations. It is an opportunity and responsibility that you must not take lightly. You have an obligation to grow the human currency along with the actual dollars in your business. Keep your people green and growing. You are positioned perfectly for this task. You are the leader. You might even learn something useful for yourself.

## Be decisive.

∽

*Ever notice that "what the hell"*
*is always the right decision?*
—ANONYMOUS

I would think that most of you would agree that the velocity of change in the business environment is accelerating at an unprecedented rate. The economy may slow, sputter, and speed up, but the rate of change has the pedal to the metal. Penetrating change and the deluge of information has overwhelmed the current global business environment.

I have observed many business leaders become frozen at the wheel trying to digest the avalanche of data cascading down upon their business, industry, and markets. Thank the information age. Some leaders have become obsessed in knowing all that they can possible know in order to make the perfect decision. Forget that notion. You cannot possibly adsorb it all. General George S. Patton Jr. said, "A good solution applied with vigor now is better than a perfect solution applied ten minutes later." It is only going to get worse because no hand is reaching for the faucet. Give it up. Do not become an information junkie. Gather what you need and take action.

You no longer have the luxury of elaborately beta testing the South Sector for six months before you bring an idea to your market or company. Times have changed and are changing constantly at an ever increasing rate. If you wait for all the compelling evidence before you make a move, you will witness your idea brought into your market by a competitor who had a more expedient decision-making process. "One of the things that I think leaders have to do—leading companies, leading people—is to see things before everyone else sees them. When something is obvious, it may well be too late," says Carly Fiorina, former CEO of Hewlett-Packard. Now more so than ever before, decisiveness is king.

From *The Book of the Samurai* by Hagakure comes this insight:

*In the words of the ancients one should make his deci-*
*sions within the space of seven breaths. Lord Takanoba*
*said, "If discrimination is long, it will spoil. Lord*
*Naoshige said, "When matters are done leisurely, seven*
*out of ten will turn out badly. A warrior is a person who*
*does things quickly." When your mind is going hither and*
*thither, discrimination will never be brought to a conclu-*
*sion. With an intense, fresh, and un-delaying spirit, one*
*will make his judgment within the space of seven*
*breaths. It is a matter of being determined and having*
*the spirit to break through to the other side.*

I am experiencing many owners, CEOs, presidents, and
leaders actually holding their breath (forget about taking
seven), hearts in their throats, lungs hyperventilating push-
ing the implement button and off they zoom. I find many
highly successful entrepreneurs and rapidly rising companies in this group. Most thriving CEOs are gathered here.
You need to be somewhat of a warrior, a modern-day samurai. Everyday could be your *High Noon.* You are Gary Cooper,
in your corner office armed with modern technology, your
intelligence, and your ability to make expedient decisions in
an unstable business environment. If not, you should be.

When you find yourself or others off track, you need to
intervene early at this easy stage. You can usually get back on
track from here. If you allow matters to slide past the easy
stage, and hit the crisis stage, you will be facing a long and
nasty journey back to your original expectations. Your odds
of getting there are slim, slight, or not at all. The slide is
caused by indecisiveness, a lack of enthusiasm, and a limited
inventory of appropriate tools in confronting the issue.

I believe that a lack of confrontation is the real culprit that causes situations to move from easy to crisis. Few leaders wake up in the morning delighted to know that they get to have a difficult conversation with a direct report. You are nice people. We all have our own connotation of what confrontation means based upon our experiences. Speaker Pat Murray suggests that, "Confrontation is a search for the truth" and in my experience it goes downhill from there, to where somebody gets physically or emotionally hurt.

There are many models of confronting. Let me share one that is a hybrid of a more sophisticated process. It has numerous variations. This confrontation model is most appropriate and effective at the easy stage. Pick your fights. Decide what is important and what is justifiable to just let go. Formal intervention is not appropriate for all situations and for all personality types.

*Intervention lite*

- This is a big person (you), little person (them) exchange.

- The intention is to get the project back on the rail and moving forward.

- This is a developmental process, not punitive. Be firm but be user friendly.

- This is a stress-less exercise and you do not lose sleep over the pending confrontation or feel like throwing up as it approaches.

*The set-up*

Inform your direct report that you would like to see him/her in your office at 10:30 a.m. tomorrow for about ten minutes to discuss his/her performance on the XYZ project.

Your employee knows that he/she is busted.

When your employee comes into your office, instruct him/her simply to listen and demonstrate the universal stop hand sign (traffic cop) as a reinforcement signal in case he/she wants to engage in a dialogue. Your direct report will want to chat. Do not allow it.

*The monologue from you*

- Explain what happened without any judgment or blame. Stick to the Jack Webb facts. Be specific. Do not gunnysack events from the past.

- Explain how this situation is affecting you relative to your feelings and emotions (angry, sad, disappointed, frustrated, bewildered, and so forth.) People cannot argue your feelings and emotions. They can argue your opinions and beliefs.

- Explain your personal contribution to this situation. Be accountable. (For example, "I failed to keep my one-to-one meetings with you.")

- Demand an immediate back-on-the-track written action plan from him/her.

- Schedule a follow up meeting (within two days) to discuss the plan, corrective actions, and accountability. This is an expanded meeting with a two-way conversation.

- Get back to leading the organization.

While playing organized baseball, my hitting coach made it simple. He said, "See the ball and hit it." There is no time or space to intellectualize the situation or to look at all the possible options. "Stay ahead in the count," he emphasized.

The same fundamentals apply in this example. See the problem, issue, situation, whatever, and deal with it in real time, otherwise you will fall behind in the count, and the advantage goes to the opponent. Ouch, strike three, and you are out!

Whatever decision you make or actions you desire, major or minor, be certain that the implementers clearly understand your expectations. What specific outcomes do you want? It has been my experience that when projects, goals, tasks, strategies, assignments go off course, slide to the crisis stage, or fail to reach completion, it is usually because the leader did not establish crystal-clear expectations with the people responsible for implementation.

Do not rely upon your direct reports to ask for explicit clarification. Many of them will not take that step for fear of looking foolish, ignorant, or for lacking the skills to complete the task. You must determine if your employee has the skill sets, knowledge, and experience to be successful. Can they do the work? Does their past performance indicate proficiency in this particular area? Are you handing off to the right person?

Be certain that the assignment is given to a person that demonstrates a willingness to complete what was started. Look for closers. Uncompleted actions generate stress for you and the employee. Check out attitudes, motivation, commitment, accountability, and determination. Consider his/her past record of accomplishments that solidify and highlight these behaviors and traits.

Establish checkpoints or project gates to pass through for evaluation of what has been completed up to a certain point and to provide an opportunity for course correction and further direction if necessary. You and the employee must make agreements that will carry the project through to completion.

It is your duty to make certain that the people responsible for the completion of your edicts understand fully what you want them to do. Invest the time upfront and do not assume that they know or should know.

Following are guidelines for setting expectations and establishing clear outcomes with your implementers:

- Explain thoroughly the task and/or outcome. Go snail, slime trailing slow, and avoid the quick time-saving, result-eroding tactic of asking, "Are there any questions?" People are usually too embarrassed to answer with any degree of truthfulness and publicly confess to their boss that they do not know how to do what you are asking them to implement.

- Explain in full detail the intent and reason behind the task.

- Ask them to give you verbal feedback, in their own words, what they perceived they heard you say regarding intent and outcomes. Listen intently for clarity, not for their memorization ability.

- Determine if they have had past experience regarding the assignment. They need to embellish and bring forward what worked for them in the past and ask for coaching if they have had limited experience.

- Ask what resources they believe they will need to be successful and to complete the project on time, on budget, meeting expectations.

- ◆ Inquire and determine how they desire to interact with you and others during the lifetime of the project. Make agreements.

- ◆ Insist that they will raise their hand high above the borders of their cubicles when they need help. Do not allow them to expire within the confines of their own insecurities and lack of experience.

There is much to cover. Do not shortcut the conversation. Do as thorough of a job as possible on the front end and you will find that the decisions and the assignments that you make will have a high success rate.

Talented, highly motivated people want to work for a leader who is decisive, who takes action, and who has forward accelerating momentum. Bottom feeders want to work for a leader who procrastinates, who mulls over decisions forever, and who is stuck. It is lonely at the bottom and they want company. You make the choice, it is your net worth and compensation package at risk.

## Set the corporate compass with *your* vision.

We should agree upon what is a corporate vision. I have facilitated many two-day, off-site, strategic planning meetings with management teams that initially cannot decide upon a commonly accepted definition. Much time is wasted with these unnecessary discussions. Some believe it is an elaborate tapestry that portrays all aspects of the company's future, others believe that it must be all encompassing, embellished with color, motion, sound, and texture. Many believe that it defines what an organization does relative to their employees, customers, vendors, board members, investors, local community, and anyone else that is remotely connected to the business. A few think it is something leaders and employees hallucinate over after far too many after work cocktails, or perhaps they have had a personal encounter with one of the many deities roaming the universe.

I allow the conversation in the sessions to continue briefly before I intervene. Strategic planning sessions need a strong, influencing hand to keep the agenda accelerating. I like to keep things simple. A vision is a significant goal that you want the organization to reach at some point in the future. It is your *tour de force* for you and the organization. A vision is an achievement that will benchmark your career and a point in the history of the business. It precedes and demands action. An old Japanese proverb suggests, "Vision without action is a daydream. Action without vision is a nightmare."

I prefer that it be specific and singular in nature. It is a BHAG, a big, hairy, audacious goal. An example of a vision would be what John F. Kennedy declared in the early sixties relative to a staggering and faltering United States space program. His vision for the space program was to place a man on the moon and return him safely to earth by the end of the decade. He initiated the vision, it was specific, significant, and singular in nature—and it worked.

It is the leader's prerogative to unilaterally establish the vision and be able to change it without going through committees attempting to make certain that everyone in the organization agrees and feels good about it. If you do change the vision, be certain to inform your people so they are working on the correct initiatives. Do not outrun your headlights.

You do not have the luxury of unproductive time by pursuing every employee to build consensus.

Consensus assumes that all managers are created equal in the eyes of good strategic decision making. It suggests that all employees at the conference table are at eye level. Other spins on consensus are "agreement, consent, accord, harmony, and compromise." "Compromise" sends shivers up and down my spine. The organization chart may suggest equality in terms of title, compensation, and benefits, but reality needs to prevail. Consensus seeking opens the door for potentially the weakest link on the team, with the most stamina, biggest agenda, and the loudest voice, holding the group and the leader hostage, and decelerating the creation of value.

We encounter business sound bites that promote getting everyone on the same page, enrolling the players to get onboard, having employees all move in the same direction, marching in lock step and all the other sayings that seduce leaders into thinking that they are doing things right by promiscuous inclusion. All of this sounds delightful until the reality of subversive behavior, power plays, sabotage, delay tactics, personal interests, and selfishness intersect with the leader's desire to do the right thing for the business.

As a leader of your business, I suggest that you seek collaboration. Collaboration suggests "teamwork, partnership, group effort, cooperation, association, reliance, and relationship." As a management team, you are going to thoroughly discuss the issue and make a decision whether to move forward. The leader has the right and duty to make the final decision if a stalemate exists. Those players who are not onboard must pledge their support for the success of the issue and join hands with the rest of the team to succeed. Down the road, if there is any indication of sabotaging by the dissenters, then that is where the leader should send those saboteurs. Besides, it is your company, your net worth, and your comprehensive compensation package.

I am constantly surprised that many leaders of organizations are content with just bumping their businesses along, hoping to bang into something and subsequently identify it as their vision. "This is exactly where I wanted it to go and precisely what I had in mind," they exclaim to the gathering bewildered employee base. Nonsense! Productive people want to be led by decisive leaders who know where they want to go and are not afraid to declare their desires. Put your stakes in the sand. Your most successful colleagues do.

Ralph Lauren believes "A leader has the vision and conviction that a dream can be achieved. He inspires the power and energy to get it done." That is known as empowering and delegating. It is your dream and you need to enlist and motivate the troops in order to reach it. It is about the doing, not just the declaring. Joel A. Barker states, "Vision without action is merely a dream. Action without vision just passes the time. Vision with action can change the world." From most perspectives, the world is a large place to impact, but I know you can influence what happens within the walls of your organization. I know you can significantly influence your segment of the market. I know with the proper vision and conviction, you can make a difference regarding your net worth and financial security.

Learn to articulate consistently. If people in your organization are chronically confused about where the business is going, it is your doing. People interpret you and your actions through their own filters and perspective, not yours. You had better make sure that they are hearing and seeing what you want them to hear and see. You might check in once in awhile instead of assuming they get it or waiting for a signal that they are headed for a deep and treacherous ditch.

Make certain that your lyrics (words), dance (body language), and melody (tone), are in exact alignment with the message that you are conveying to your implementers. Be accountable for your words, actions, and demeanor. They are yours. Keep your message simple. Keep the conversation focused. Baseball great Yogi Berra said, "It was impossible to get a conversation going; everybody was talking too much." Keep the insignificant chatter at a minimum.

Most successful leaders are absolutely consistent and relentless in keeping their vision visible. Every encounter with their employees is an opportunity to embed their vision into the thinking and activities of the implementers. No gathering of employees is too small for their vision stump speech. No space is too sacred to escape the message about where they are going. You know you are about to reach saturation point when an employee sees you coming down the hall and suddenly ducks into the nearest restroom. Gender is irrelevant. Follow the employee in, check for feet under the stall door, knock, and lay it on them one more time, "What have you done today to accelerate us toward our vision?"

"Successful communication transforms your thoughts, will, and desire into action. It moves people. It transforms the thoughts, will, and desires of others. What better word for this process than magic?" says Jack Griffin, author of

*How to Say It at Work.* Spin a little magic and see how pristine, persistent, and consistent you can make the communication of your vision.

## Drive the business with *your* principles.

Elvis said, "Values are like fingerprints. Nobody's are the same, but you leave 'em all over everything you do." I have never considered The King to be much of a philosopher (You ain't nothing but a hound dog? What?), but I believe he captured what I want to say in this section. He is right. Many organizations choose to consciously and deliberately execute their principles when it is comfortable or convenient, but their fingerprints are left behind in all instances. In the end, organizations are known for what they stand for rather than for what they sell. Recently, Enron, Tyco, WorldCom, Martha Stewart, and others appeared on the major network's six o'clock news. These behemoths of global commerce and their leaders will be remembered for what they slumped to, not for the products, goods, or services they provided or the heights that they reached. These embedded impressions have a long shelf life. Nobody is able to go back and entirely wipe clean the crime scene.

Business expert Ken Blanchard said, "Identifying the core values that define your organization is one of the most important functions of leadership. The success or failure of this process can literally make or break an organization." He has plenty of company. Henry Meyer III, Chairman and CEO of KeyCorp, reinforces further the notion of values by stating, "The best-performing companies are managed by those who walk the talk. Here at Key these values drive everything we do. Ethics are not just words on pieces of paper. Values aren't merely posted on a door. The shadow cast by leadership is the starting point for how our values cascade down from the top so that they permeate the culture and can be felt by everyone we touch."

Let me share what successful businesses leaders are doing relative to this issue of principles and values. I witnessed these firsthand. There is not much wiggle room in this discussion and if I ever came close to declaring absolutes, this is it.

**Absolute number one: This is your domain.** The principles that you lead your organization with must be authored and originate from you. I do not believe this is a democratic process or should be sent to committees for a decision. It is your right to establish what you believe is appropriate for your business and not be held hostage to a group's declaration or desires. The principles that you hold dear propelled you to where you are today so they must work just fine. Make what you believe in highly visible. Be extremely explicit. Communicate, communicate, and above all else, communicate.

**Absolute number two: Remember, you are in the fishbowl being observed constantly and judged critically.** Below is a line from a song made popular by Sting.

> *Every move you make,*
> *Every vow you break,*
> *Every smile you fake,*
> *Every claim you stake,*
> *I'll be watching you.*

—from "Every Breath You Take"

How true. So now, you are warned. It may not be fair but it is reality. Stay awake. Stay conscious. You must be impeccable in setting the example of how you want these principles and values lived and carried out. Screw up out of sight. If you are busted, fess up—do not cover up!

**Absolute number three:** Keep the principles few in number and high in impact. You are not in the behavior modification business. Fuggetaboutit. You cannot create the perfect employee. Keep it simple and decide what is really important and meaningful.

I was actively recruiting a prospective client in the Northwest. This CEO was successful, high profile, and a fast tracker in the pharmaceutical industry. As I was waiting in the reception area of his business to interview him, I could not help but notice the ten-foot by ten-foot value statement placard that was secured on his lobby wall. It was that enormous because he had posted twenty-three values that he expected his employees to embrace. I thought to myself, "slight overkill." When I met with the prospect, I mentioned to him that there were only ten original suggestions bought down by Moses, and we as a world community over the past 2000 plus years were having considerable difficulty implementing all of them to any acceptable degree and perhaps he could scale his back just a touch. He eventually did and became an active client.

**Absolute number four:** Live your principles always—especially in the following three instances:

◆ **When you hire a new employee.**

◆ **When you witness your principles being executed.**

◆ **When you witness your principles being ignored.**

People walk into your organization with their own embedded software. Some prospective employees are team players—others may be lone wolves. Some are honest, some are crooks, and the list and possibilities goes on. If a corner-stone value in your organization is teamwork, you would be foolish to hire a lone wolf who takes no prisoners while blazing his/her own trail. You had better interview for the trait that you desire inside your walls. The odds suggest that the past is the best predictor of the future. Investigate if this prospective employee has this attribute and experience inside of him/her. If you hire someone with the wrong internal software and later attempt to convert him/her, you will be subjected to something similar to a real software conversion. You know the drill:

◆ **It will take longer than expected.**

◆ **It will cost more than quoted.**

◆ **It will not work as advertised.**

Be smart. Hire people who have the same values that you have.

When you witness the company values being lived by an employee or a group, make it visible. Call attention to it. Celebrate. Reinforce it. Broadcast the event to the rest of the organization. Do whatever is necessary to drive the message deep into the hearts, souls, and behaviors of the people in the business. You must be relentless in your effort. Posting the principles on some poster or screen saver and thinking that will steer the message home is naive and mostly unproductive. You do not affect people at any significant level by sending out an effective-immediately memo that the business is a team-based organization.

Equally important is making visible in real time any violation of the principles. Turning your back on any erosion of what you hold as important diminishes what you believe in and says to the organization that these values and their implementation are arbitrary, optional, and ultimately impotent. Believe what you stand for and stand for what you believe. You are not running a popularity contest, and if you have a high need to be liked and allow your employees to run roughshod over your values, you need to spend more time with your therapist.

**Absolute number five:** Use your principles as a filter for decision making. This is your first cut regarding any choices or decisions that are made in your business. It precedes strategic, economic, synergistic, logistic, and all other considerations. Roy Disney suggests, "It's not hard to make decisions when you know what your values are." These values create the crucible where the work takes place. The crucible must be solid, able to hold up under stress, enduring, and above all else, provide safe and predictable boundaries for people to do the work that you hired them to do.

## Delegate, and get busy doing what you are paid to do.

In my third year of facilitating CEO groups, the light bulb suddenly went on. The issues we were discussing in our monthly meeting were management concerns, not exclusively leadership topics. Duh! I had allowed the group to dumb down. I put this matter on the following month's agenda knowing that potentially I was going to have to fall on my own sword.

At the next meeting, the group and I had a frank discussion about how we were spending our time and what we were bringing to the table to discuss and advise. It was all about return on time and resources. We concluded that the subjects that we were investing time, money, and intellect in were mostly items that should have been delegated to the members' management teams and not be cluttering the agenda of fifteen leaders of fast-growing companies. I had a room full of carnivores and we were spending our valuable time chomping away on veggies and cream cheese. We were traveling along at ground level when we should have been soaring at 30,000 feet looking over the horizon.

Following our discussion, a two-foot by ten-foot blue and white vinyl banner hung on the front wall of our meeting room stating:

## These Leaders Work on CEO Stuff

The sign became a reminder to always be mindful of their roles in their organizations and where true leaders should be working and focusing. Robert Halk reminds us, "Delegating work works, provided the one delegating, works."

In order to execute the fine art of delegation you must consider the following:

◆ **What am I willing to let go of?**

◆ **Do I have anyone to hand off to?**

Until you become clear on these two items, I would stay put. Scrub the list of the activities that you do on a daily basis and decide what is appropriate for you to do and what is not. Be honest with yourself and determine from the following reasons and excuses why you are doing what you are doing.

Reasons and excuses for not delegating to key reports (managers):

- Of all the people on the organization chart, you are best suited to do the task. (*This often happens in start-ups, but look for a handoff.*)

- The task has become habitually unconscious and is now a part of the corporate woodwork. (*Get conscious and make an appropriate assignment.*)

- You flat out like to do the task. (*Okay, I can buy that for a short while.*)

- You are a control maniac and micromanage everybody and everything in the organization. What you do some of the time you do most of the time and you are probably driving your family crazy. (*You need an immediate control-ectomy and serious counseling.*)

- You have decided, in the name of expediency, that it is faster and more opportunistic to just do the task yourself. (*You will never have a life and your "bench" will never rise to the task.*)

- You are in the wrong slot on the organization chart, still consider yourself a manager, and should go to work for another company. (*Read all the leadership books, watch all the DVDs, attend all the seminars, and see if you will ever qualify.*)

◆ You are in a chronic talent-impaired condition and have no one to handle the non-CEO tasks. *(You will soon encounter CEO burnout and lose a good percentage of your hard-earned equity as you tumble down the backside of your bell shaped curve.)*

Refer to the beginning of this chapter and match your daily activities to what I defined as the role of an effective business leader. You know what is the right thing to do. Consider the following:

◆ **You will have to spend some money.**

◆ **You will have to relinquish some control.**

◆ **You will have to let go of some of your pet tasks.**

◆ **You will have to move some people in and out of the organization.**

◆ **You will have to get out of your comfort zone.**

◆ **Most important, you must assume the right and proper role in your business so that it may thrive and prosper.**

Remember, you deserve it.

Gary was a member of my CEO group for four years before I turned it over to a successor. He is still with those CEOs and I hope he remains for years to come. They need him. Gary personified everything that I have discussed in this chapter. Gary earned his MBA from a prestigious Midwest university. He is a hired gun leading a business in the $150 million range, growing the business at fifteen to twenty percent annually and producing profits that are approximately four to five times the industry average. He is a hot property and could run any business in any industry and be successful because he absolutely gets it.

I spent hundreds of hours with Gary picking his brain and exploring his success. Here is what I discovered about him. He is the billboard for everything that we have discussed on leadership. Gary realized that his people are the key to his success. His next in command is potentially better than Gary. He rejoices in making the decision to hire him. He has made certain that all of his key reports have access to him at a personal and professional level. He spends a high percentage of his budget on training his people in the skills and behaviors that will move them and the business forward.

Gary is the most effective and intentional communicator that I have ever encountered in the business world. There is no ambiguity in his statements. The organization knows where it is going because Gary keeps it in their top-of-mind awareness. He is not embarrassed or shy about being redundant and repetitive.

Gary allows his direct reports to run their portion of the business; however, when decisions are stalled or need to be accelerated, he takes full command. He makes few decisions, but the ones he makes are courageous and of high impact.

There is no hiding the pea when is comes to this leader's principles. All who come into close contact with Gary understand clearly where he stands. The organization is recognized as the leader in its market segment and Gary is recognized nationally for positions that he has taken in a tumultuous, bureaucratic, and highly regulated industry. His strategies and decisions are always value-based. He sleeps soundly at night. His family comes first, his business farther on down the line. I would like for all of you to meet him. You would be better for it.

**Review:** To be a successful and effective leader of a business you must:

1. Own the leadership role.
2. Inspire, influence, and transform your people.
3. Be decisive.
4. Set the corporate compass with *your* vision.
5. Drive the business with *your* principles.
6. Delegate, and get busy doing what you are paid to do.

**Robust actions to take:**

1. Who in your organization do you need to spend more shoulder-to-shoulder time with developing their skills, behaviors, and leadership abilities?

2. Define your vision for your organization.

3. What decisions are you procrastinating on making?

4. What explicit principles do you want to make visible to your organization?

5. What tasks and responsibilities are you willing to delegate to another person?

# 4

## STRATEGY FOUR:
## Value Resiliency Over Brilliancy

*Ya gotta do what ya gotta do.*
—SYLVESTOR STALLONE

∽

## Get over "it" quickly.

AS THE LEADER OF AN ORGANIZATION facing unprecedented change and challenges, you do not have the luxury of
throwing a prolonged pity party. You need to work through
adversity quickly. You cannot go down with the *Titanic*. There
are too many passengers and crewmembers depending upon
you to make the right move. Get in the life raft, bark out some
articulate, explicit orders, and start paddling. The company
stands on your shoulders. The company is made of your stuff.
You are the corporate warrior that others will turn to for guid-
ance when you ram bow first into an unforgiving iceberg.

Former NBA basketball great Pat Riley said, "Each warrior wants to leave the mark of his will, his signature, on the
important acts he touches. This is not the voice of ego but
of the human spirit, rising up and declaring that it has

something to contribute. In every contest, there comes a moment that separates winning from losing. The true warrior understands and seizes that moment by giving an effort so intense and so intuitive that it could only be called one from the heart." Unpleasant, unpredictable events are going to happen to you and your company in this postmodern business era. That is a given. Are you up to it?

You are not firewalled against misfortune. There are no moats between you and impending catastrophe. JP Garnier, CEO of GlaxoSmithKline suggests, "Resilience. It's the number one quality you need today to be a CEO. I have a lot of smart people who couldn't last in this job. It's about being hit and being able to stand up again, because the job of CEO is mostly bad news coming across your desk." Key employees are going to leave, bankers are going to unexpectedly call loans, competitors are going to steal customers, governments are going to tax you unfairly, and occasionally you are going to have a miserable day with your bloody nose flattened deep into an unforgiving and abrasive canvas mat. By the way, it hurts like hell!

Being off-the-charts brilliant, creative, innovative, a team player, a strategic thinker, and a consensus builder is not going to get you through all of those moments. It may have secured you an "A" in one of your graduate business classes, but that was years ago in a synthetic and unrealistic environment. Resilience is your hammer now. Adversity and unanticipated setbacks are the nails. Resilience is singularly your greatest strength. Get up off the mat, wipe off the blood, and make something happen. Let me illustrate what resiliency means by examining the true-life personal and business adventures of CEO clients, Emily and Derek.

Emily completed two years of college and went to work for a firm in a service business. She was bright, ambitious, and willing to work. She learned quickly what she needed to know and in her midtwenties, along with a male partner, she acquired the firm that had hired her and suddenly found herself an owner, CEO, and beholden to the bank. The personal guarantees were something that most of you would not expect. She did not. Her ascension was fast and not quite anticipated. It was a meteoric rise; intellectually exhilarating, financially risky, and it kick-started her on a journey as a leader of this and future organizations. Facing a slippery, vertical learning curve, she grew the business, made numerous rookie mistakes, and survived through tenacity, hard work, and a little luck.

After a few years of difficulties, starts and stops, internal power struggles, circling, and competing in a rapidly and ever-changing business environment, the company settled into a predictable routine and made steady progress. Just when events were moving along smoothly, the industry suffered a downturn, her male partner turned into a testosterone-injected predator, and Emily found herself on the short end of a naive and ill-conceived buy-sell agreement. She was young and inexperienced. Unexpectedly separated from the company that she helped grow and minus any sizeable return on the investment, she deemed it all a good learning experience. Youth and unbridled optimism will do that.

Out on the corporate mean streets again with a scuffed up ego and an excellent reputation in her market segment,

Emily was immediately recruited and hired by a regional leader in the industry. She found herself plopped in the president's seat as a high-profile major player, back on her feet and upright. Vertical is good.

She reported to the owner/CEO who now wanted to devote more time to another project and be free from the day-to-day operations of the parent company. Emily was suddenly in the big leagues facing big league challenges and considering major league opportunities. She was wearing new pinstripes and they felt a little tight in places.

Barely in her thirties, she was neck deep in an extremely competitive market, working for a demanding and highly-recognized CEO, fighting an organizational structure that had the owner's custom stamp deeply branded on it, facing employees who were fiercely loyal to the former leader and who were dedicated to maintaining the status quo. Would you have taken on this challenge?

Emily had challenges in both her professional and personal life. As the business demanded a majority of her focus and energy, her marriage began suffering from neglect and unresolved issues. She suddenly found herself working late into the dinner hour attempting to put her imprint on the organization while trying to salvage a teetering and fragile relationship.

Unbeknownst to others, Emily was also at war with a substance abuse problem. She was drinking far too much, much too long, and entirely too often. Chardonnay had quietly and persistently captured more of her waking hours than at any other time in her past. She was functional but suspected that she was headed for trouble. She was. She is bright. She is conscious. Emily rationalized that her position as the designated leader of a prospering, well-recognized organization demanded that she entertain existing customers and prospects, that she have a presence at citywide social events, and be available at the drop of a hat for postwork gatherings with her new staff to bond and build trust with them. It all seemed reasonable to her from her presidential leather chair. These occasions involved drinking and her alcohol consumption continued to rise. It seemed manageable, but in reality, it was taking a toll on her energy, self-esteem, and spiritual life.

Faced with leading a challenging business, returning home late in the evening to a faltering marriage, and experiencing a frustrating and an accelerating alcohol usage, Emily had to regain control of her life and immediately extinguish her self-inflicted brush fires. Life, she was beginning to learn, is about choices and consequences. We read that in self-help books but seldom does it hit the sweet spot until it happens to us and suddenly we get it.

She went to work with intent, conviction, and renewed energy. On the job, Emily did the best that she could with what she had at her disposal and what she could control internally. The owner struggled with letting go of the company. Emily's efforts to move the organization toward her were consciously and unconsciously sabotaged, or subtly put on the back burner by the CEO. In spite of the tacks in the road before her, over time, she won the hearts, souls and minds of her inherited and newly-hired employees, terminated the weak and nay-sayers, established firm financial controls, set a clear and passionate vision, opened new markets, grew the

business in both revenue and profits, and performed com-
mendably. Her scorecard was in the black.

While all this was taking place, she and her husband were
attending counseling sessions to determine whether they
could salvage their relationship and build from that platform
into the future. It was taking an emotional toll on both parties. If that were not enough, Emily enrolled voluntarily in an
outpatient alcohol rehabilitation program that demanded her
participation in evening group therapy sessions twice weekly for three hours thirty miles from her office for the next six
months. I am on overload just writing about it. She never
missed a day at work, never skipped a counseling session
with her husband, and her attendance in the rehabilitation
program was perfect.

That was the good news. The rest of the news was that
eventually she was unsuccessful in keeping the owner out of
her stable and she was slowly and consistently losing her
reins on the company that she was hired to lead. Recognizing
the bold handwriting chiseled on the corporate wall and realizing her inevitable fate, Emily resigned gracefully, leaving
the organization better than when she was hired. It was a difficult, and in her thinking, a one-step-backward decision.
The counseling sessions with her husband led to a painful
but mutual decision to dissolve the marriage. Emily graduat-
ed from the alcohol rehabilitation program and joined a
professional women's AA group. She has remained clean and
sober ever since.

No job, a lost marriage, and a lack of an alcohol escape
mechanism, up off the mat she rose, a little bruised, a bit bat-
tered, but armed with her integrity, intelligence, resilience,

and an expanded wisdom. Emily agreed with Harrison Ford, the actor who said, "I realized early on that success was tied to not giving up. Most people in this business gave up and went on to other things. If you simply didn't give up, you would outlast the people who came in on the bus with you." She immediately reset, wrote a business plan for a new venture, furthered her education and due diligence by attending international workshops on the industry, and launched her infant company. That is being resilient. It was a privilege to be at her side.

## Understand that resiliency is your differentiator.

Daniel Goleman in his book *Emotional Intelligence* states, "One source of a positive or negative outlook may well be an inborn temperament; some people by nature tend one way or the other. But, as we shall also see, temperament can be tempered by experience. Optimism and hope, like helplessness and despair, can be learned. Underlying both is an outlook psychologists call self-efficacy, the belief that one has mastery over the events of one's life and can meet challenges as they come up. Developing a competency of any kind strengthens the sense of self-efficacy, making a person more willing to take risks and seek out more demanding challenges. And surmounting those challenges in turn increases the sense of self-efficacy."

Stanford psychologist Albert Bandura states further that, "People who have a sense of self-efficacy bounce back from failure; they approach things in terms of how to handle them rather than worrying about what can go wrong." Kathleen

Noble, Ph.D., in an article entitled "Gifted Women: Identity and Expression" wrote, "Resilience is a tri-fold process of recognizing and resisting the intrinsic and extrinsic obstacles that inhibit the development of one's potential…the way you go about enhancing resilience is to first of all recognize how critical a psychological factor it is."

My experience with successful leaders is that not only do they have the ability to tap into a high percentage of their human potential, they have an abundance of self-efficacy that springs from both the inherent and experience well. Regardless of its source, it is a deeply embedded component of their makeup and a robust tool to leverage that provides them an extraordinary advantage over their competitors. They seldom back off when situations are not going their way. While others are licking their wounds and feeling sorry for their latest plight in life, these winners seize the opportunity to capitalize on other leaders' prolonged recovery periods. They are up off the mat and moving forward to the center of the ring where the action takes place.

Remember many of you do not have a team of professional handlers (the seasoned MBAs) in your corner, applying wound-healing ointment, snapping open smelling salts, and giving you a swig of mountain fresh spring water. You are sitting on a corner stool alone, facing the turbulence and wiping off your own eight-ounce padded gloves. The referee is going to call you to the center of the ring and the fight is going to continue for many more rounds. Are you going to answer the bell? It is a choice of throwing in the towel or getting off the stool.

Therefore, it does not matter if you were born with resilience or you acquired it while leaning back against the ropes doing your version of the Ali "rope-a-dope." If you want to be successful in leading a business, resilience had better be a part of your repertoire.

Derek had created a holding company of six operating units threaded together by a loosely defined common mission. He had hired or retained professional managers to run the individual businesses, consolidated accounting and other administrative operations, and empowered his managers to make decisions and operate independently. His control was distant, noninvasive, and in retrospect, too hands-off. He totally trusted his managers to keep him informed on the health of the businesses through his COO and to involve him only in major decisions. At the time, it seemed like the right concept. It almost brought him down.

Unbeknownst to Derek, the COO of the holding company withheld information for ego purposes, control needs, and a lack of his own off-the-resume talent. One dark and stormy day in Derek's life, it almost came apart. A prominent unit in the portfolio was in dire trouble. The business was hemorrhaging cash, was over-inventoried, and managed poorly. This had been going on for months and had been shielded from Derek's view by the COO. Derek had allowed his businesses to be leveraged much too far, stretched too thin, and to be controlled by others. The troubled company was putting the remaining units at risk along with Derek's hard-earned net worth. Derek admittedly had considerable accountability in this unfortunate potential outcome. Do not we all. Ah, the webs we weave.

Keeping in mind that the darkest hour is only sixty minutes long, he stepped into the skirmish and took command.

For Derek, the challenges were both exhausting and unexpectedly exhilarating. He felt betrayed. Immediately, he fired his COO. Over the next year, he sold off the assets of the troubled company, renegotiated his financial situation with his bank that had changed hands several times, hired a new CFO, and grabbed possession of his cash flow. On the road, he consistently visited the five remaining operating companies, resetting their plans and establishing unfiltered communication lines with the operating managers.

In his early sixties, slightly overweight, quadruple bypass scars crisscrossing his chest, Derek put in long days and nights on the road and at the office. He was meeting with lawyers, customers, accountants, advisors, and bankers while dealing with the day-to-day and long-range stress of keeping the businesses intact and preventing his relatively small financial empire from collapsing. At times, his wife, peers, and I all worried about his physical and mental health and wondered whether it was it worth the pain and aggravation. He obviously thought it was and with determination, he plowed on.

His peers advised him on numerous occasions to put the businesses on the market, pay off the remaining debt, and to get on with his life. That was a reasonable solution and according to most everyone's opinion, it would eventually work. The numbers panned out. There would be ample capital left over after the debt was retired to do whatever he wanted to do. No way, declared Derek! He adopted the old Japanese proverb, "Fall seven times, stand-up eight." He stayed vertical. Vertical is good.

At times, he looked and felt like those inflatable, bottom-weighted clown punching bags that once socked keep popping back up, daring you to take another punch. He never stayed down for the count.

Eventually the businesses stabilized. Derek is now in the process of re-evaluating where he wants to go and what he wants to do with his life. He did his best to keep events and issues in perspective. Like best-selling author Robert Fulghum suggests, "If you break your neck, if you have nothing to eat, if your house is on fire, then you got a problem. Everything else is inconvenience."

My friend, you are going to make mistakes. That is a guaranteed reality. If you do not think you are going to blow it now and then, you are either an incredible genius immune to human frailties, terribly arrogant, or in absolute denial. Resiliency is what is going to pull you through to the finish line. A little brilliancy also helps.

## Download resilience into your organization.

You might be resilient, but how do you get the organization to go there with you? Besides acting quickly and using resilience as your primary tool, I am going to share with you the strategies and actions I have observed leaders and organizations implement when faced with difficult times and seemingly insurmountable challenges. You might be next, so sit up, and pay good attention.

Most successful business leaders are able to:

- ◆ **Make their personal resiliency unmistakably visible.**

- ◆ **Create a strong support group around them.**

- ◆ **Be willing to do something different.**

- ◆ **Throw intelligent and appropriate resources at the obstacle.**

## Make your resiliency visible.

In working with business leaders, I have concluded that for the most part, organizations mirror the characteristics and state of their leader. So go you, so goes your business. I do not believe that opposites attract as much as I believe that people like to be around others just like them. Remember being "aware and beware" of the fishbowl? Your employees are watching you from sunrise to vespers, and among many other things, they are trying to emulate your positive behavior. At the very least, your productive keepers are observing. You have a running start at creating a resilient organization just by being highly visible day-in and day-out. Make bold moves in full view of your organization. Take responsibility, make what you do evident, and see how much resiliency you can rub off on your organization. It is like super glue.

In a May 2002 *Harvard Business Review* article entitled "How Resiliency Works" written by Diane Coutu, she says, "Resilient people possess three characteristics: a staunch acceptance of reality, a deep belief that life is meaningful, and an uncanny ability to improvise. You can bounce back from hardship with just one or two of these qualities, but you will only be truly resilient with all three. These three characteristics hold true for resilient organizations as well." Without question, the resilient leaders I have worked with had an abundance of these three qualities.

One of the first CEOs to enroll in my CEO group was Sid. He is a large, orangutan-like man with an enormous heart, laugh, and outlook on life. One of his favorite sayings is, "It just ain't no big deal." He is able to look at life that way because he searches for the truth in all situations instead of escaping to the safety net of denial, fantasy, opinion, and self-delusion. He understands that the truth is much easier to deal with than denial and fantasy. It is upright and ultimately undeniable. Challenges are not big deals to Sid because he approaches each one with a reality-based humor, unwavering optimism, and resolve. Sid is a scientist by education, a business owner by choice, and an incredible free spirit by incarnation.

Every February Sid and his wife travel to the Big Island of Hawaii, rent various types of lodging, and settle in for thirty frolicking days away from the business. It is how Sid takes care of himself. Variety is essential for this particular business leader, so each year he chooses a skill or an expertise to become proficient at and that is his focus for the one month. One year he learned how to weave baskets; another time he invented and manufactured nonalcoholic liquors; a recent vacation found him researching and devising a treatment program for his wife who had been stricken with breast cancer. It was always interesting for us to hear his latest project.

I started each monthly CEO meeting with what I term an inclusion exercise. Each member updates his colleagues on significant professional and personal activities of the previous four weeks. It is a way of connecting after a month-long separation. As the roundtable discussion progressed, it was Sid's turn.

"Well, let's see," Sid began looking down at the list he had prepared as prompts. "In February, Joan and I took our annual trek to Hawaii. While there, I learned how to play the harp. Very difficult instrument to play, I might add. The business

ran fantastically in spite of me not being there. In fact, we
had a record month. I just might stay away much longer next
year. Let's see. Oh, while we were gone, our waterfront house
burned to the ground, destroying everything that we had and
leaving only a smoldering motor block in what used to be the
garage. Everything was up in smoke. Our grand kids...."

"Err, ah...hold on just a minute, Sid," I interrupted. "Did
you just say you lost your house and all your life's posses-
sions and it burned to the ground while you were on
vacation?"

Sid looked up surprisingly from his list and said, "Yeah,
but it just ain't no big deal. It happened the first week but
there was no need to come back. Hell, nothing was left so
what was the point? Besides, I was just starting to get the
hang of that bloody harp. You know it was time to get some
new stuff in our lives anyway, never was that crazy about the
house, and I figured it was just the universe's way of telling
me to stop being so complacent and to get going again. We
have plenty of insurance so it will all work out fine."

We all leaned forward in our chairs slightly stunned at
what we had just heard. Most of us were thinking, "How can
he be so lighthearted over what most families would consider an absolute tragedy? Sid, what about the freaking family
pictures?"

That is vintage Sid. He keeps events in perspective, tries
to see the good that might come out of an incident, and real-
izes that the only outcome he can control is his reaction to
what is happening. He takes the high road; eyeball-to-eyeball
he stares reality down and gets creatively busy. In this
instance, Sid focused on the bigger picture and realized that

no real harm had occurred because no lives were lost or endangered. He keeps life's circumstances inside parameters so that he can deal with them effectively. He planned on replacing and upgrading the damaged and destroyed belongings. His spiritual foundation allows him and Joan to look at the event as an opportunity for new beginnings, fresh adventures, and letting go of the past.

Six months later, Sid was enjoying a new single-story home on a different low bank waterfront lot, a cactus-inspired Southwest interior decor, and current family photographs perched throughout the home. Joan's cancer was in remission, and their new wardrobes hung in their new closets. Life and "it" just continues to go on.

As Diane Coutu suggests, resiliency is about being real, looking for meaning in circumstances, and doing what you have to do in innovative ways. Sid's peer group observed their colleague, his employees watched their leader, and we all learned firsthand in real time what resiliency looks like.

## Create a strong support group around you.

Resilient people do not do it all alone. They have figured out that they can only stretch themselves so far before they eventually unravel. When unexpected challenges knock on your door, call in the team and even the odds with whatever you are facing. This is not the time for taking "macha and macho" stances. Rally the troops!

In an afternoon session with my CEOs a few years back, a shaken veteran member brought up the following issue for advice and solutions. Dan was a local manufacturer in the perishable food industry. He had well-branded, gourmet quality products that sold well at both local and regional retail grocery outlets. Unfortunately, after a long-term, seemingly healthy relationship, one of his major customers dropped his product. Overnight, without any overt warning, he lost 25 percent of his business. It had vanished. That really hurts. As a business owner, something like that gets your attention and tends to spoil your day.

The group worked on the issue for the remainder of the meeting. Dan admitted that perhaps he had gotten a bit complacent, lost contact with the account while food brokers represented his products, and he was not paying as much attention to his revenue stream as he had in the past. Comfort and familiarity had prevailed. Dan had become unconscious and had fallen asleep. The conversation with the group revealed that the lost account was not about price, service, sales, quality, or anything that was obvious. All that Dan knew was that he was losing his slot on their shelves along with considerable sales and profits.

In the meeting, we suggested a multitude of strategies, discussed contingencies, and before the day was over, Dan left the meeting with a well-thought-out, streamlined game plan on how he was going to weather the financial turbulence and regain the account. His peers helped him to "chunk down" the problem and focus on those two vital and essential outcomes, which kept him from being overwhelmed and thereby diluting his resilience. It was a start, and there would be many revisions as the conversation continued. A renewed bounce in Dan's step propelled him out the door and down the steps as we adjourned the session. He got the help that he needed and he was not facing this in isolation.

Because Dan admitted to becoming a bit lackadaisical in his leadership, one of the mandates of the group was that whatever he decided to do, he had to answer to his colleagues on an ongoing basis. He was to keep us up to date on his activities, tactics, and movement. Not only were we going to hold him accountable on implementation, but we were also going to be there for him emotionally, spiritually, and physically as he faced the two daunting tasks of winning back the mega account and staying above his financial waterline. "Lonely at the top" is an archaic notion and a poorly-conceived term. We were not going to let Dan go down on our watch.

Dan declared war on the situation and led the troops, but not too far out in front. He kept his employees well informed of what was happening. They had strategy, brainstorming, and small town hall meetings to dispel rumors and to eliminate obstacles that might surface. He sought additional advice and support by forming an advisory group, separate from his CEO peers. This team roster consisted of an accountant, a lawyer, a vendor, and other professionals in his industry. Dan surrounded himself with people who could assist him in moving through this setback. He rallied loyal customers to see how they could help in resolving the setback. He had his advisory support teams in place to assist him in meeting the challenges ahead and to boost his confidence. He called in various chits and favors that were within his reach.

### Be willing to do something different.

Dan's two primary objectives were to stay healthy financially and get back on the shelves of the regional grocery chain. Being resilient does not mean being stubborn and to keep firing the same shells at the same target. That approach is more like being persistent. Our colleague needed to consider, explore, and implement new tactics. Over the years, Dan had sold his products through food brokers or with in-house sales people, which had been a highly successful approach. That was then but this was now. The food brokers had been calling on the buyer and making no progress. The buyer denied an audience with the brokers who now could not penetrate the account through the traditional existing channel. A different and creative approach was needed.

Apple Computer founder, Steve Jobs, suggests that "Innovation distinguishes between a leader and a follower." Dan, taking the lead, decided to become the primary contact man with the account and he returned to an earlier strategy that he implemented when building the business. He became the Chief Sales Officer and personally worked the account.

Through his reputation, position, and relationships, he was able to meet with the leader of the lost account. The meetings were cordial but noncommittal. Dan did not learn anything new or gain much headway, but he respected the leader's decision to let his buyers run their segment of the business. Respectfully keeping doors open, Dan had to try a different, more effective strategy. With his financial well-being and net worth on the line, Dan kept plugging away with the resources he had available. He kept existing communication lines open to the leadership, managed his cash the best that he could, and kept pursuing new business.

While all of this was taking place, a groundswell of customers was building up on the shores of the retailer wondering where their favorite product was and what was this other product doing on the shelf? Questions, concerns, and requests bombarded the buyer demanding the return of the product. Some customers threatened to take their business to competitors. Articles appeared in industry publications and local newspapers about the sudden and mysterious disappearance of Dan's products. What was occurring was a pull-through strategy in forward gear and it was working better than anticipated.

Barry Diller, CEO of IAC, reinforces the concept of doing something different, "I'm never absolutely sure of anything, and I don't want to be. You're either right and you'll pull through, or you're not. We're never going to be right about everything, and we've certainly been wrong."

After approximately one year of major account drought, Dan had a surprise visit from one of the leaders of his former customer. He asked that Dan come back, reclaim his slots, and let what had happened in the past be long gone. Restoring his shelf space and the relationship, Dan returned to his old customer. He had simply stayed on the bus.

## Apply intelligent and appropriate resources to overcome the obstacle.

When faced with company-threatening adversity there is no reason to hold back resources. Let us review what Dan set in motion to overcome his setback. Dan:

- **Became real about the situation and recognized the immediate impact it had on his business's cash flow and his personal net worth.**

- ◆ **Did not allow himself to be isolated in facing the problem.**

- ◆ **Established accountability with his peers.**

- ◆ **Kept respectful communications lines open to all parties.**

- ◆ **Became personally invested in solving the problem.**

- ◆ **Kept it simple by focusing on two primary objectives.**

- ◆ **Called in overdue chits.**

- ◆ **Did not burn bridges nor leave a scorched earth.**

- ◆ **Tried a new and different approach.**

- ◆ **Buckled his seatbelt and stayed on the bus.**

You will have your own version of this. I am not suggesting that this is the absolute, hands-down, guaranteed model for working through business speed bumps, but it worked for Dan and is a possible template for you.

I believe that good businesses get better in bad times and bad businesses no longer record a recognizable blip. Good businesses get better because their leaders keep them from disappearing into the La Brea tar pits of dinosaur companies by remaining resilient and teaching their organizations to be likewise. Dan attacked his problem from a variety of fronts by keeping actions and strategies simple, straightforward, and concentrating his limited resources on the two specific outcomes of profitability and regaining the account.

I have never been a fan of the David and Goliath one-sling, one-rock strategy. With limited resources at hand, I want low-cost options in my arsenal launching from multiple strategic positions. Optimism and resiliency suggest that somewhere under all that horse crap there is a pony in there.

I believe that this resiliency characteristic is your trump card. Do not underestimate it. Play it for all it is worth. Stay on the bus, keep looking through the windshield, and resist the temptation to follow the crowd and flood the exit doors as soon as "it" gets a little testy. Resilience has gotten you to where you are and it still has a long and productive shelf life.

**Review:** To be a successful and effective leader of a business you must:

1. Get over "it" quickly.
2. Understand that resiliency is your differentiator.
3. Download resilience into your organization.
4. Make your resiliency visible.
5. Create a strong support group around you.
6. Be willing to do something different.
7. Apply intelligent and appropriate resources to overcome the obstacle.

**Robust actions to take:**

1. Currently, what is the most challenging "it" in your business?


2. What are you doing about it?

# 5
## STRATEGY FIVE:
## It is All About The People

*I get satisfaction of three kinds.*
*One is creating something.*
*One is being paid for it. And*
*one is the feeling that I haven't been*
*sitting on my ass all afternoon.*
—WILLIAM F. BUCKLEY

∽

### Understand that extraordinary people create extraordinary results.

WE HAVE BEEN GIVEN BAD ADVICE. Recently there have been several experts suggesting that you can get extraordinary results out of ordinary people. Nonsense. Extraordinary people manufacture predictable and consistent business results. Business leaders seldom experience an outstanding corporate result in spite of their employees. The ultimate success in any business depends upon the quality of the human currency within the walls of the organization and by sitting the right butts in the right seats at the right time. A great plan, strategy, vision, or clever and brilliant leadership seldom survives an ultimate head-on collision with a low DNA factor. Mangled strategic plans, loss of bottom-line profits, frustration, and wasted, unproductive time fill that intersection.

I will admit that during certain critical circumstances, seemingly ordinary people rise to the occasion to produce unbelievable and unanticipated outcomes. Occasionally, the ball is stripped clean of its cover and sails into the grandstands. Specific emergency events often prove that extraordinary performance is possible. They are mostly physical accomplishments and not strategic business moves. If I am sitting in the corner office of my business, I do not want to wait for the adrenaline to start surging through the veins of my direct reports and the sirens to start wailing before my management team rises to the occasion and bails the business, my net worth, and my annual compensation out of harm's way. It does you little good to be passing by the accounting department and hear someone suddenly shout, "Clear!" If I am leading an organization, I demand daily, consistent, predictable high performance, and I assure you it is not going to come from dull steak knives in your corporate drawer or elevators that do not go all the way to the presidential penthouse suite.

I am not telling you anything you do not know. It is just that once in awhile you suffer from an unanticipated acute amnesia attack and try to do what you do completely alone or with limited human resources. You then sit back in wonderment and utter disbelief observing that the project failed or imploded on the launch pad. It is good to have rocket scientists on your team during design, lift-off, orbit, and re-entry.

You know the problem; for many of you, the most talented people in the available employee marketplace pool are not lined up outside of your Human Resources director's door, if you even have one, begging to go to work for you. There are good, productive people queuing up seeking employment and opportunity with your organization, but not the same caliber crowd who are FedExing their resumes to Fortune 500 companies and to the other behemoth competitive players. You usually attract, and ultimately hire, second and third tier talent. Unfortunately, that is a fact for many of you.

There is a way to increase your odds of attracting and hiring extraordinary talent. I am going to share with you what I have observed your most successful colleagues do to boost their talent pool and give themselves a competitive edge. Pay close attention.

## Make it your priority to proactively recruit, hire, train, and retain extraordinary talent.

It is not always easy but it is always essential. Most companies, especially below the giant level, approach these personnel tasks on an emergency basis. When the need raises its ugly head, you become instantly active and frantically start the game of catch up. Under those circumstances, it is often too late and usually not very effective. Get proactively in front of this issue and approach it strategically as if it were of utmost importance. It is. Try implementing strategies, completing tasks, reaching goals, being creative, and building your net worth with minimum and questionable talent. That formula guarantees disappointment and chronic leadership heartburn.

When facilitating strategic planning sessions with companies, I usually insist that the number-one priority be securing and retaining extraordinary talent. It is a good business strategy for me because I am confident that the plan that I help create for the organization has a high probability of being implemented, thereby assuring ongoing future business with that client.

Systemize this process. Make your system for dealing with talent highly visible, well-thought-out, thoroughly understood, and consistent throughout the entire organization. Keep evaluating what is working and what needs just tweaking, or a major up-on-the-hydraulic lift overhaul. Do not fall asleep when it comes to your people.

You have spent countless hours and have invested considerable dollars in creating systems and processes for manufacturing, invoicing, collecting receivables, sales management, inventory control, and all other functions of your business. Most of you approach the people issue with malignant casualness and benign neglect. It deserves better. I know that some of you believe that if it were not for all those damn people running around your plant or office that you just might get something done. That dictates an immediate attitude adjustment. People are not going to go away, so figure out how you can deliberately and strategically approach and maximize your return on this essential resource. You must become an expert in understanding human beings. Good luck!

## ABR: Always Be Recruiting

This should be the mantra of your Human Resources director. There is a good chance you do not have one, but if you do, and he/she has a wideband skill level, elevate this position from compliance, benefit packages, and touchy-feely personal counseling, to being the VIP in charge of procuring talent. It is not enough for the Human Resources director to keep the "sue-the-company-for-free-bulletin-board" bombarded with all the latest threats and edicts from the government and labor unions or to devote his/her activities to fulfilling the role of mother-father confessor. I just hate that when it happens. This job is and should be more all-inclusive. It is your direct channel to extraordinary talent. That should be the number-one objective and primary focus of your Human Resources department. Why settle?

If you do not have an internal Human Resources function in your business, then outsource it to a contract firm that specializes in all the extended and inclusive activities of a true professional in Human Resources. Do not drop it on your controller's or CFO's shoulders. Remember, for the most part, people and their nagging, petty issues are irritating to financial types. Consultants in this field have informed me that the magic number is 100 employees, and at that point Human Resources comes in-house along with a hefty salary and comprehensive benefits. Do what works for you, but in any case, redirect your entire workforce into HR advocates, and all of you participate in implementing **ABR**. You must lead the charge.

Keep a talent warehouse file handy. Consistently fill that folder with the business cards and resumes of talented people whom you and your employees encounter in your world. If the person selling you a new cell phone makes a favorable impression, ask for his/her card and have a brief conversation about your company and potential opportunities. Develop a well-rehearsed, articulate, compelling, and convincing stump/elevator speech. Keep in touch. All of your managers should do the same so you have an active and current inventory of prospects to **ABR**.

Be imaginative. Bring your best and brightest people periodically together to create and implement strategies to increase the talent quotient in your business. How can you best upgrade? You do this when considering other business matters, so why not with people? Winners like to be with other winners but not necessarily in the same department or on the same horizontal line on your organization chart competing for the next open slot on the company's food chain or for capturing that outstanding performance bonus.

Please understand that there is one inherent and predictable problem. You are the only person in your enterprise who will aggressively and deliberately hire someone better than you. Your managers will swear on the Bible or the Koran while saluting the American flag, that what I have just suggested is not even close to the truth, that they would have no issue whatsoever with personally recruiting and hiring a person that is smarter, more talented, better dressed, more handsome/beautiful, or with skill sets far beyond their own. Do not fall for that one. Watch their nose for immediate prolongation. No one is deliberately going to create terminal obsolescence for himself/herself. You need to be the lead dog. It is the best view.

## Hire fast, fire faster

Put considerable thought and action into how your organization is approaching the issue of hiring extraordinary talent. At one time, I bought into the popular notion of "hire slow, fire fast." That was a good and logical sound bite when the velocity of change in the business world was chugging predictably along. You, as the leader, had the luxury of thoroughly investigating whether a potential employee would be a decent fit with your organization. There was ample time to contemplate, interrogate, investigate, integrate, and implement all the other "ates" before making a decision on any specific candidate. This approach does not work as well now as it did in the recent past. You still need to do all the "ates," but you need to do them more quickly, with more intensity, and with more intention.

Hire fast, fire even faster is now more appropriate. To accomplish this, it is imperative that you have a streamlined, well-thought-out procedure that accelerates the decision-making process regarding people both coming and going. If you, or your direct reports, drag your heels in making decisions on hiring talented and terminating untalented people, you are going to come in second place. First place is more fun.

In this free agent environment, the winners have more options and an abundance of suitors more so than ever before. Top organizations have figured out how to move people quickly through decision intersections, keep them tethered to the mother ship and to get them on board. It must be a smooth, expedient, and effective journey from employee candidacy to the first day in the cubicle. Interruptions and snags in this process allow penetration by other suitors. Identify all the gates that a prospective employee must pass through, organize the process, and keep streamlining for effectiveness. Here are some of the gates you need to construct and maneuver through effectively.

- ◆ **Investigate and select a suitable testing instrument that provides you with a penetrating and revealing look inside the person you are interviewing.**

Go once, go deep, and be quick. Time is ticking. If you are waiting for weeks for the results of the test, you do not have a competitive chance. Remember that people walk into your organization with their own embedded behavioral software and you had better make certain that it is compatible with the cultural and behavioral software in your organization. You are not and never should be in the behavior modification business. It is not your expertise. How successful have you been doing this with your teenage daughters and sons? You love them, they love you, and you still cannot get it done. Give it up and hire people who demonstrate the qualities that you desire inside the walls of your business. Test for it.

- ◆ **Design and implement a consistent, repetitive, and effective, interviewing methodology.**

Invest in training your existing employees on how they can effectively and efficiently evaluate prospective candidates during the interview. A cynical part of me believes that hiring is a crapshoot regardless of what you do, but let us put some deliberate thought into this most important function and do the best that we can to place the odds more in your favor.

There is an art and science in productive interviewing and you need to investigate and decide what allows you the best chance in determining whom you are bringing into your organization. Remember that once in, they are difficult and expensive to extract.

I have observed firsthand ineffective interviewing. Here is how it usually goes.

Interviewer says, "We here at Acme Manufacturing believe that teamwork is an essential ingredient in our success. Tell me, do you believe that teamwork is essential?"

Prospect replies, "I believe it is the only way to be successful in any organization."

Duh! Well, excuse me. The candidate would have to be a world-class, out-of-the-box, blithering moron or an unemployable relative to answer that question in any other way. As I said before, the past is the best predictor of the future.

The interviewer should have said, "We at Acme Manufacturing believe that the cornerstone to our success is teamwork. You have an impressive resume and certainly possess the skill sets that we require. Please share with me a time when you were on a high-performing team at your previous job, what was the team all about, what you accomplished, and what was your contribution? I would also appreciate, if you would (compliance issue), the names of your teammates, their telephone numbers, and e-mail addresses. Take your time, this is important."

I will ask and I will check if given permission. I demand compatible software. Put the odds in your favor. Tomorrow I will have someone else in the company interview this candidate and ask the same questions. Afterward, we will huddle and compare notes. The truth is easy to remember and lies are often difficult to consistently recall.

♦ **Be willing to open up your pocketbook a bit wider
   and deeper to pay for talent.**

Like most everything else in life, you usually get what you
pay for. Do not be a tightwad. I was having a one-to-one with
Mike, a CEO client, and before we started, he had to show
me the new machine he purchased to increase productivity
and streamline production. Out onto the manufacturing
floor we rushed. He was full of vim and vigor, enthusiasm
and passion, excitement and confidence.

I found myself standing before a $3-million, computer-
driven, high-speed gizmo that was guaranteed to increase
productivity, reduce expenses, and deliver at a speed never
before imagined. Mike did not have a clue to how this mar-
vel of modern technology actually worked, but he bought
into its benefits and agreed to pay the asking price.

As we walked back to his office, we passed the littered
cubicle of Frank, the bookkeeper, who was methodically
preparing the monthly profit and loss statement counting
revenue and expenses on his fingers and toes. Mike was full
of resignation, passivity, and disinterest. Frank only cost this
CEO a visible $40,000 a year in salary, but I wondered how
much was the real price?

Mike considered his bookkeeper a financial bargain, but
was he really? Many of our one-to-one conversations centered
upon Frank because his financial reports were chronically
late, he was not much of a team player, seemed preoccupied
in detail, and never really participated in shaping the company's strategy. In addition, he seldom worked with the banks,
passing off that responsibility to the owner. Frank was not up

on the latest financial management software, but he was cheap, familiar, and had been there a long time.

I question what keeps leaders from investing in people at the same scale and confidence that they invest in tangible assets. Where do you stand in this decision? What do you value the most? What prices are you paying for discounting the contribution of your people to your success? What are you willing to pay for extraordinary talent and peace of mind?

## Train to retain your winners

Effective training, challenging assignments, and retention of your best people go hand in hand. Pay close attention. It costs employers 50 percent to 150 percent of an existing employee's annual fully-loaded salary to hire their replacement. Search efforts, training costs, loss of productivity, and stalled momentum escalate the expense of losing key people. You must become focused on doing something about this extremely costly and company-threatening condition. Keep your game breakers.

Winners currently view themselves as free agents, owners, and investors. That is an unprecedented mindset. It is a new ball game with new rules and requires a different approach by leadership (that's you).

As free agents, the "30-year gold watch employee loyalty scheme" is long gone from both the employer and employee standpoint. The allegiance between employee and employer has diminished from both sides. Highly talented people are more mobile, more willing to seek and respond to opportunity, and more visible in the marketplace than ever before. Thank the digital world and the information age for that. You are fortunate if you can corral talent for four to five years before they move on to a more enticing offer or initiate their own startup or acquisition.

As owners, they demand the opportunity for personal and professional growth to increase their inventory of skills, wisdom and knowledge, which they carry within them wherever they eventually land. That is where a comprehensive training program and challenging assignments are essential and come into play.

Seeing themselves as investors, they realize that the more they own, grow, learn and expand their skill, knowledge and leadership abilities, the more valuable they become in the marketplace as investors seeking a higher comprehensive return on investment for what they bring to the corporate conference table. My mentor, Jim Jensen, suggests that your goal as an employer is to assist your employees to become better all-around people, not necessarily just better employees. They just might recognize that this is important and spend a few more years with you. Remember "balance?"

Enter into the conversation with your key people. Stay current with the folks who are making you successful. Do not be held hostage by them by trying to satisfy unreasonable and selfish demands, but do determine what it will take to Velcro them to your organization for as long as possible. Regardless of what you hear them say or watch them do, they are ultimately tuned in to an FM station with the call letters WIIFM broadcasting live from deep within their personal needs and considering the question that matters most to them, "What's In It For Me?" You will need to negotiate to a "win-win" result to answer that question. You should never be surprised or caught off-guard by the sudden and unexpected departure of one of your winners if you have engaged with them in a candid and ongoing developmental dialogue. Keep the conversation current.

## Get rid of deadwood.

This gets a bit tricky for a couple of reasons. First, not many people who lead companies enjoy waking up in the morning knowing that what they must do that day is terminate an employee or two. Second, the primary strategy of deadwood is to stay off the corporate radar screen and be difficult to detect. Get over the first one and know the second tactic does not work that well either. People are known by the company they keep, and companies are known by the people they keep. Who are you keeping that you should not be? What is it costing you financially and emotionally? How does this reflect on your business and you as the leader?

I want to make one thing clear. I am not a "chainsaw" fan. I believe it is right, fair, and proper to give people every opportunity to succeed. You must provide the resources, mentoring, clear expectations, and support your employees need to accomplish their objectives. Make certain you have them in the right seats doing what they do best. Foster an attitude of wanting them to do well and then do what is necessary, within reason, to assist them in reaching that outcome. When they demonstrate that they are incapable or unwilling to step up and display behavior that is unacceptable, then it is time to turn them loose and for you to get some well-deserved sleep.

Keep in mind that you must take every opportunity available to consistently upgrade the talent in your organization. Turn this seemingly stressful dismissal into a positive, proactive action and not a heavy, negative burden. You are making the right decision even if you are tossing and turning all night and feel like throwing up.

I realize that going through the process of firing an employee is not an all-encompassing pleasant experience. The majority of you are nice people and "executing" an employee causes stress on your over-sensitive psyche. Get past it. Remember that at times it is easier and less stressful to change people than it is to change people.

As a speaker colleague Will Phillips says, "Value honesty over niceness." What is your niceness costing you and the organization? The honest approach is for you to confront the dilemma and to act promptly within the guidelines of your value system. You are probably the only one losing sleep regarding this. It will not be as difficult as your imagination has projected. Why do most of you go to worst-case scenarios when it comes to people?

The marginal, equity-eroding employee sleeps peacefully each night knowing that he/she has successfully stolen one more day on the job and eagerly accepted another "company welfare check" from you. Thank you very much! That is the truth and you all, at some level, know it. The day after you actually "make someone available to industry" as my friend, Red Scott, a Horatio Alger Award winner, describes this activity, your door is filled with employees asking you why it took so long.

So why does it take you so long? What are your excuses for jeopardizing your hard-fought net worth and financial security? Here are a few of the classic, imaginative excuses and unreasonable reasons that I have heard:

- "I didn't notice it because I was busy doing other things." (*Denial strategy*)

- "I thought it would work itself out." (*Divine intervention strategy*)

- "It is their manager's responsibility, not mine." (*Not-accountable-pass-the-buck strategy*)

- "The timing is not right." (*Procrastination strategy*)

- "The devil I know is better than the devil I don't know" (*Head-up-your-rump strategy*)

- "But I know the family, in fact, it is mine." (*Poor-genetics-Catholic/Jewish-guilt strategy*)

- And many more. (*Unlimited rationalization strategies*)

I consulted for a brief period with a CEO of an international public company that, in my estimation, lopped off people in a cruel and ineffective manner. Annually, he and his numerous direct reports participated in a mandatory, two-day, off-site "slaughter." The drill consisted of subjectively evaluating their employees one through however many there were, with no two employees occupying the same slot. Being number one was great; being in the bottom 10 percent had some vulnerability problems. The managers had to include themselves in the ranking while excluding the CEO. He was no dummy.

Immediately upon returning from the off-site meeting (Monday morning) the bottom 10 percent would be summoned into their manager's office, handed a blindfold and a cigarette, and told to have their desk emptied by the time the sun set that day. In full view of their relieved peers, a security guard would escort them out the door with a banker's box over-flowing with pictures of their children, personal belongings, and other company memorabilia tucked tightly under their arms. Security, the Human Resources director, the payroll clerk, the bottom 10 percent employees, and their department managers had a busy and extremely excruciating day.

Can you imagine the anxiety and turbulence that was created in that organization, as the management team pulled into the company parking lot after their "lost" and perhaps "last" weekend together? Is there any way to determine the cost associated with the loss of focus, productivity, and morale of this organization as the employees anticipated the retreat, waited for their score and the accompanying summons to see the hangman that Monday morning? Now there is a hell of a way to start your week.

Step into the shoes of the Human Resources director and the challenges of rapidly implementing mass terminations and replacing employees from various departments. Think about the liability and exposure to subsequent wrongful termination lawsuits, sexual and age discrimination complaints, and possible complications caused by a lack of documentation and personnel paper trails.

The CEO was blind to all of this vulnerability and believed that this was a fantastic idea that he obtained from one of Jack Welch's books and that it was a useful strategy to raise the level of performance and talent in his organization. Maybe it worked for Jack but it did not work so well for this JW knockoff. While Jack moved on with his stock options, corporate jet, and New York apartment, our enlightened boy was left with paranoid employees, low morale and an organization that failed to attract extraordinary people with high self-esteem. Eventually we parted company, as did many of his talented people. It was crowded at the exits. This is not a good model unless you have extraordinary talent lined up and pounding on your door. Do not do it.

Be compassionate when removing the deadwood, but extricate it. You either directly or indirectly hired or inherited them, so you have direct or backdoor accountability. You also played a cameo role in their lack of success in conscious and unconscious ways. Again, get over it, and please do not set them up for life with an overly generous severance package to soothe your guilt. This is not fun but it needs to be done. That last sentence rhymes and will make it easy to remember.

## "Show and tell" them that you care.

"I literally trust you with my life. This business, that I created, is my life and if I didn't care deeply about each one of you gathered in this room, I would never consider relinquishing the control and power that I ultimately used to have, to all of you. I am and have been over the years handing my fate over to you. You're the primary reason for my success. You know that, don't you?" Randy's eyes began to moisten as he spoke to his management team while concluding a two-day strategic planning retreat that I was facilitating. His voice was soft, his speech unexpectedly uneven, and the message curiously unfamiliar.

This highly successful owner/CEO was, for the first time in his 25-year career, explaining to his managers what they all meant to him and how important they were to his life, success, and peace of mind. Collective gulps and sighs could be heard from this highly attentive band of frontline managers.

He had been to their birthday parties, attended their weddings, occupied a front row seat at their first-born baptisms, and celebrated with them as they moved up the organization chart. Randy sponsored company picnics, hosted Christmas parties, and said hello to his staff as he roamed the halls of his organization. He assumed that they must all be aware of his interest level in them as individuals. He assumed that they all knew how much he trusted and cared for them. Surely, his actions spoke much louder than his lack of words.

Assumptions can be misleading. Now, as he was about to step out of the everyday leadership of the company that he founded, he made it official as to how much he valued the people who worked for him and contributed to his good fortune. His management team, perhaps for the first time, really got it. It was not too late but it was late.

Richard Farson, author of *Management of the Absurd: Paradoxes in Leadership* says, "Caring is the basis for community, and the first job of the leader is to build community, a deep feeling of unity, a fellowship." Make it official early on in the game. Your people will go to extraordinary efforts if they sense that you really do care for them. They need to know and you need to make it explicit. People want to know that others value and are concerned about them. Go far beyond the generally expected. It is sound business. Be genuine. This is not the time nor the place for empty, trite platitudes and synthetic expressions of caring and concern. High-performance people have acute bullshit detectors, so be sincere.

When I was playing organized high school and intercollegiate sports, many of my coaches would periodically ream me and my other teammates up one wall and down another for a performance that was not up to their established standards. We would be chastised, criticized, and humiliated both in private and in full view of our relieved colleagues. We called it being "ripped a new one." By the way, that hurts emotionally. Following the "feedback" episodes, we were informed by the righteous coaches that they certainly would not have behaved in that manner had they not cared for us so much. Right!

Be thoughtful and appropriate when expressing your care and concern for your employees. People process information according to their individual filters, not yours. You want the message to be heard and understood fully, so you might have to customize your delivery depending upon the recipient and the situation.

Please make certain that you do the following:

◆ **Spend scheduled, quality one-on-one time with your keepers.**
  *Robust actions I will take:*


◆ **Give them continual developmental, not punitive feedback.**
  *Robust actions I will take:*

- Challenge them with interesting, stretching assignments and keep raising the bar.
  *Robust actions I will take:*


- Go out to a restaurant/event with them and pick up the tab.
  *Robust actions I will take:*


- Write them personal notes of congratulation (not e-mails).
  *Robust actions I will take:*


- Publicly and privately, acknowledge their outstanding performance.
  *Robust actions I will take:*


- Design a career path with them.
  *Robust actions I will take:*


- Coach, mentor, and role model.
  *Robust actions I will take:*


- Help them to align their goals with your business goals.
  *Robust actions I will take:*

- Criticize the performance, not the performer.
  *Robust actions I will take:*


- Follow up with them on agreed-upon personal and professional outcomes.
  *Robust actions I will take:*


- Always be a trusted and enthusiastic advocate of their self-esteem.
  *Robust actions I will take:*


- Above all else listen, listen, and listen.
  *Robust actions I will take:*


- And much more (start with how do you want to be cared for and valued).
  *Robust actions I will take:*


I heard Dr. Phil tell his television audience that to show others that you really care for them, you must challenge and support their commitment to do what they need to do to have what they want to have. That makes incredible sense. How committed are you and how are you demonstrating it? I want you to be in a professional relationship with a person playing that role in his/her life. It is good business and there will be rewards. Go do it.

**Review:** To be a successful and effective leader of a business you must:

1. Understand that extraordinary people create extraordinary results.

2. Make it your priority to proactively recruit, hire, train, and retain extraordinary talent.

3. Get rid of deadwood.

4. "Show and tell" them that you care.


**Robust actions to take:**

1. What are you going to do to raise the level of talent in your organization?


2. What do you need to do to be more proactive in recruiting, hiring, training, and retaining extraordinary talent?


3. What do you need to do to extricate the deadwood in your organization?


4. What are you going to do to express care and gratitude for your employees?

# 6

## STRATEGY SIX:
## Understanding Your Numbers is Not Optional

*Cash ain't cash unless it's cash.*
—RED SCOTT

⌒

**Remember that you are in
business to make money.**

IT WOULD BE NICE TO PICK UP THE CURRENT *Wall
Street Journal,* turn to the financial section, scan the quarterly
report on XYZ Corporation, and discover that your favorite
company is a good and gracious community neighbor, that
the organization provides wonderful perks, comprehensive
benefits for their employees, makes substantial annual con-
tributions to local charities, and so on. Unfortunately, the
reports are revenues, earnings, price-to-earnings ratios, market capitalization, and a multitude of other revealing, stark
statistics. What I really wish that I could do is buy a *Wall
Street Journal* one day in advance of its publication. A fellow
could make some real money doing that.

I must remind you, and you must continually remind
your employees, that the primary reason you are in business

is to consistently, and in an ethical manner, make money. Lots of cash. Period. End of story! No other acceptable options come first. It is not about realizing your ultimate dream, continuing another generation of a family business, being independent, or anything else. All of those reasons are important and honorable, but you will not have an opportunity to experience any of them if you do not deliberately subordinate those outcomes to being vibrant financially. Everything else in your business comes in second place except your principles, for they determine the manner in which you ultimately secure your profits.

The scorecard (your income and cash flow statement, your balance sheet) reports the statistics and metrics that indicate whether you and your employees are allowed to come to work the following morning. Remember what educator and writer Laurence J. Peter said? "Don't knock the rich. When did a poor person give you a job?" You can create and implement all that other feel-good stuff once the profits are accounted for, secured, and safely deposited in your corporate vault.

Keep this one thought in your top-of-mind awareness. Everyday it is your net worth, your equity, and your annual compensation package that is always at risk with every move you and your managers make. You need to focus on and create a consistent vertical ascension in profits and revenue to stay vigorous, active, and alive in the game of being in a business. Gather, interpret, and understand what the numbers of your business are saying to you. They tend to shout loud and clear if you are listening and paying close attention. If you are not attentive, you are surely lost and riding steep down-hill rails to a nasty train wreck with your net worth and financial future dangling precariously from a narrow gauge railroad trestle. Far below, the gorge is cold, ambivalent, and does not give a hoot whether you succeed or fail.

## Pound your financial stakes in terra firma.

Financial management is another system in your business. You need to treat it as such, and intentionally, consciously, and deliberately decide how you want it to be. Do not make it up as you and your employees move along on your journey. If you are reading this book, there is a good chance that you have climbed up your ladder past the I-don't-know-if-I'm-going-to-make-it stage. The experimenting should be over, and by this time, the financial approach to your business should be in the ever-evolving, refining, tinkering phase, and no longer a dipping into the cigar box, making-it-up-as-I-go-along start-up tactic.

What are your fiscal goals? How are you going to measure them? What systems do you need to install and implement to reach your identified financial objectives? What is your strategy? What are you doing to educate yourself and your employees on sound monetary management? What is your budgeting process? How do you communicate the financial health of the organization to your employees, your bank, and the other share and stakeholders? I have many more questions for you to consider but this is a good start. You still have orders to get out the door by this afternoon.

My most successful clients were clear on the following:

- What the organization needed to do relative to its continuous financial health.
  *Robust actions I will take:*


- What percentage growth rate they wanted to grow the business.
  *Robust actions I will take:*


- What the industry financial standards were and how they matched up with their company's fiscal results.
  *Robust actions I will take:*


- What percentage of sales or actual dollars they established as goals for their various margin lines.
  *Robust actions I will take:*


- How much debt or cash was required to maintain or grow the business and at what interest rate.
  *Robust actions I will take:*


- How regularly, with what content, and in what form did they want their financial reports to land on their desks.
  *Robust actions I will take:*

- ◆ What they wanted defined in the budgets, how the process was implemented, and how people and departments were held accountable.
  *Robust actions I will take:*


- ◆ What they wanted the value of the company to be when it was time to take hard-earned chips off the table.
  *Robust actions I will take:*


Think through these questions and make them essential elements in your strategic and operational planning. Create financial strategies, goals, and actions that accelerate you and the organization toward the stakes. Hold those who are the implementers accountable for hitting the specific targets. Identify the key performance indicators that reveal the stark truth about who is contributing to the financial health of the organization and who is not. Provide them adequate support so they may succeed. Establish definite consequences for those who continually come up short. Make visible the progress or lack of movement toward the goals. Implement immediate actions to correct the situation by declaring war on the obstacles. Keep a current and exact score.

## Create your box score.

When I was a young boy, I scrutinized, studied, and memorized the box scores, standings, and statistics of my major league baseball heroes and teams as reported in daily newspapers. The numbers exposed and forecasted slumps, identified winning and losing streaks, showed who was hot and who was not, and among other things, predicted trends, recorded results, and suggested future outcomes. You need, with the same enthusiasm and devoted interest of a young, fanatic, baseball nut, to do the same with your company's box score. If you fail to do this, you might be in for a long season characterized by mounting losses, strikeouts, bean balls, and disgruntled, fickle fans that take no pleasure being down in the cellar with you.

What are your corporate equivalents of at bats, hits, runs, errors, strikeouts, and walks that tell the story about your day, week, month, and year at the office? Do you have a process that indicates in a timely and concise manner the financial health of your business, or do you have to sort painfully through piles of convoluted and disorganized data from multiple sources to understand what is happening to your net worth, equity, compensation package, and peace of mind? Are the financial indicators predictive or are you examining historic information that tells you about the past but fails to give you a future-oriented roadmap or wake-up call? Do you truly understand what you are tracking and what to do with the information once it is on your radar screen?

Personally, my eyes and interest tend to glaze over and dull when examining stacks of financial information. Somehow all those columns, ratios, balances, and margin lines do not excite me as much as making a sale, motivating an employee, or giving a well-thought-out, inspiring state of the company speech. I would rather participate in an intimate conversation with another person than pour over statistics that are not linked to a local sports franchise and

highlighted in the morning's sports section. If you are anything like I am, and leading a business, you had better
quickly get over what you do not like to do, bite the bullet,
and educate yourself on sound, fundamental, financial management. In addition, surround yourself with people who do
get their jollies looking at charts, graphs, trends, and are
good communicators to boot (those are a rare breed).

If you were stranded on a deserted, tropical island armed
with a cell phone, limited minutes available, and could call
your business only once a month without being slammed
into voicemail hell, what would you want to know that
would indicate to you that your corporate doors would
remain open the next day? What financial data, in a flash,
would reveal to you the macro-picture regarding the true
current and future financial health of your company? What
information would allow you to sleep well that evening in
your bamboo hut or motivate you to jump into a dugout
canoe and paddle furiously to some appropriate destination
to initiate immediate, corrective action? What would be on
your company's flash report? That is your box score. Figure
it out and know it well.

You must custom design this snapshot. It must make
impeccable, explicit sense to you. It must tell you what you
need to know about your business, and not be so generic
that it could slide easily into any company, giving any exam-
iner one-shoe-fits-all-general information. Obviously, some
of the areas on which you will need data are revenue, profitability, and cash flow. More important, you need to
monitor the factors and indicators that affect those three
areas. You want causes, not symptoms. Perhaps you need to

track your backlog and pipeline. It might be important to monitor the number of proposals being written and submitted. Your inventory might be an indicator that you watch closely. The financials are the vital organs of your business. They keep you alive and you cannot afford to have your monitors suddenly and unexpectedly indicate that your vital signs have flatlined.

How you measure those ingredients and what individual specific twists you put on them must be restricted to your business and relative to how you personally digest and evaluate information. If you are dominant left-brain and analytical, bring on the spreadsheets and ratios. If visual, how about some color charts and graphs or a PowerPoint presentation? If you are auditory, then have someone tell you what is going on with your business backed up with printed data. Do something that works for you.

Scan all the elements that significantly make your business successful and pinpoint exact areas of importance that you need to scrutinize closely and periodically. Keep in mind that there are numerous items to review ranging from strict, hard line, financial data to company cultural and logistic issues. You make the choices.

Consider the following when setting up your specific flash report items:

◆ The items must be predictive, not solely historical.

◆ The items must be easily understood and obtainable.

◆ The items must be timely, scheduled, and relevant.

◆ Keep the items few in number and high in impact.

◆ Do not lock onto them forever. Your business may change and the information provided may no longer reveal to you what you need to know.

◆ Have others outside your business periodically and objectively review the information.

◆ Act upon the data as needed.

◆ That is enough. Now go out to lunch.

## Do not fly blind.

Imagine that you are progressing up the ladder in securing your flight pilot's license and it is now time for the dreaded, up-in-the-sky, instrument-rating test. You and your instructor climb into the cockpit and fasten your seat belts; you in the pilot's seat, an experienced teacher in the jump seat with cool, orange-lens sunglasses and leather flight jacket.

The take-off is smooth. You bank left away from the airport, level out at 10,000 feet, compass reading due north, ground speed approximately 145 mph, and wait for further instructions. Your instructor, with your cooperation, secures an opaque hood over your head and the panel before you. You are suddenly blind to the horizon and everything else that provided your bearings. All of your senses go up a notch or two. You are instructed in a firm and commanding voice to continue to fly the plane relying solely on the instruments on the cockpit panel, under your hood. As you follow the instructions, you discover that all the instruments essential for safely flying the aircraft have been painted over with black opaque paint and you cannot see the dials, gauges, or anything else relative to the instruments. It is pitch black. Sweat suddenly pours from your forehead, palms, and armpits, your insides begin to churn. Panic sets in as you realize that you could crash and burn if something is not done to immediately correct this perilous emergency.

This can happen to you in your business if you do not have current, reliable, and accurate financial information on the company you are piloting. Flying financially blind, at some point, will cause you to bury your enterprise into the ground.

In fifteen years, I had only one member of my CEO group crash and burn. It was not pretty. I have some accountability for this because I let him join as an unsophisticated business executive, leading a company that he had allowed to become chronically ill. I did not perform proper due diligence and had lowered my standards for entry. My only salvation was having a picture of what not to do. Inadvertently, we all learned from the experience.

Ralph was in his sixth year of owning and leading his own distribution business. He was generating annual revenues in the mid-seven figure range. Having survived that long creating those revenues, I assumed his financial house was in good order. Assumptions are often dangerous. Ralph's background was sales and marketing. He knew how to move merchandise from manufacturer, to warehouse, to retail outlets. His customers liked him; he was handsome, charismatic, and enjoyable to be around. Being seemingly open, a good communicator, and easy to be with, I immediately felt a kinship with him.

Welcoming him into the CEO group, I bypassed the interviewing procedure that had proven valuable to me and other prospective members in the past. I overlooked trusting and implementing the process. Owning his own company was always Ralph's dream, and barely into his forties, he had accomplished just that and was now going to sit monthly at the conference table with seasoned and successful CEOs. Welcome to the big leagues.

In preparation for his first meeting, I requested that he share with the group what they would need to know to assist him further on down the road when specific issues came to the forefront. He thought that was a good idea but wanted to take it one step further by presenting a pressing issue to the group in his first meeting. He requested some immediate assistance on one particular subject. I thought that would be fine to jump-start him into what we did every month.

We discussed the issue and the process and agreed that having the group appraise his financials would be an important bit of information in helping to resolve his temporary cash flow problems. I asked to review his income statements to better understand his profit picture and to study his balance sheet to preview his cash flow status before the group did. He explained that the October statements were not available because his bookkeeper was on vacation, but that he would have them gathered in time to show the members at the November meeting. A red flag was going up the pole and I was in denial. Bookkeeper, seven years down the road, seven-figure revenues, hmmm.

Fast forward to the November meeting. For about thirty minutes, his peers listened to a narrative from Ralph about his cash flow woes, and then spent considerable time reviewing a stack of copied documents that he tried to pass off as his current balance sheet and income statement. The data was disorganized, outdated, coming from multiple sources and software programs, sprinkled with a multitude of errors, and missing vital information. Ralph appeared shaken and embarrassed. So was I.

Ted went first. "Ralph, you seem like a nice guy and I hate to say this because I just met you about an hour ago, but based upon what you have told and showed us this afternoon your ass is grass and your banker, the government, and your suppliers are the voracious lawnmowers. You are out of business, have been for some time, and you don't seem to get it. My friend, how could you let this happen?" The room became quiet. Smiles went south as each member focused on Ralph and perhaps reflected upon their own businesses and how this might happen to them if they did not pay diligent attention to their own finances.

"This is extremely serious and unless you have an angel somewhere, you're basically toast, finished, gone." Harsh words to a new member from a veteran, financially savvy, successful company president. Ted seemed appalled. His voice was stern, his body language closed and resigned. I knew I would hear from Ted after the meeting. Our new member was not an appropriate fit. Ted did not intend to be cruel or crude, but he wanted to get this relatively new CEO's attention and to cut to the chase. Besides, Ralph was wasting our time because the situation was beyond repair and we had other members' issues to address on that November afternoon.

A chagrined Ralph shared with us that he had not had current financial information on his business for over ten months. He was too busy and caught up in performing his role of saving existing accounts and securing new business for the organization. He was not comfortable with finances. He ran the business intuitively. He had a "feel" for what was going on. He subordinated all that fiscal activity to the incapable hands of his part-time bookkeeper. He was now paying a monumental price for that choice and approach. What he thought was that money was tight and everything would work itself out in the end. After all, it always had in the past.

When he finally managed to patch something together for the meeting, he did not understand what the numbers were telling him. As a group, we did understand, but with the resources he had available, it was too late to do anything constructive. Ralph had used the group, as a last gasp effort to save his business while facing what he thought might be the inevitable truth. He was finished and that was a difficult pill for him to swallow. It would be for anyone.

The group gave Ralph good advice on how to ethically and morally shut down the business, deal with vendors, the bank, and squeeze what he could out of what he had available to him. We were all sorry that this was happening to a seemingly well-intended man. Two months later, the bank called the loan and his suppliers cut him off. Ralph sold or returned his remaining inventory for discounted dollars, tossed the business into bankruptcy, went to work for a competitor, and began once again to sleep uninterrupted through the night. It was a deep hole to crawl out of, but at the very least, he had a monthly paycheck coming.

My most successful clients did the following regarding the financial management of their organizations:

◆ Demanded that all of their financial reports be given to them on time.

◆ Insisted that the reports be accurate and inform them, in customized detail, what they wanted and needed to know.

◆ Made certain that the form in which the information reached them was understandable and consistent with how they individually processed financial information.

◆ Took immediate, corrective action when data indicated a problem.

◆ Had outsiders review their statements for accuracy and objective interpretation.

◆ Spent quality time with those providing them the reports and knew their financial people better than anyone else in their organization.

If you are not receiving your reports in this manner, then raise havoc and get everyone that you need back on your track. It is your net worth and compensation package that you are protecting and trying to expand. You deserve every opportunity to increase it. Howard Hughes got it right when he said, "I'm not a paranoid, deranged millionaire. Goddamit, I'm a billionaire." You are entitled to the same. If conditions do not improve, then make the necessary personnel and process changes and find someone who understands what you want and is committed to delivering the goods to you exactly the way you want them.

### Insist upon financial literacy.

During the open-book management craze, I witnessed many well-intended business leaders make a significant effort at sharing financial information with their employees. They had digested just enough information and process regarding this management flavor-of-the-month to be armed and dangerous. It usually took on this form. The CEO and the in-house financial guru, whether a bookkeeper, controller, or CFO, would decide upon basic financial information to share with the employees. It seemed like a good idea to let the employees know where the company stood from a fiscal standpoint so that they could play a part in improving the numbers that were being made visible. It was truly a watered down version of the total program of open-book management and deserved more attention to make the process more effective.

Periodically pinned up on the sue-the-company-for-free-bulletin board alongside all the human resources compliance notices, and government and union threats went the designated numbers. Impressive, informative, but what do they all mean? The casual observer immediately noticed that sales for fiscal year 2004 were $20 million and net profit was 10 percent. It did not take much of a self-acclaimed, financial genius to conclude that the owner had obviously pocketed $2 million and the damn tightwad would not even match the 401(k) at any significant percentage or buy the sales staff new cell phones.

If you are going to make your numbers visible to your employee base, you must accompany the information with continuous, financial literacy training. They must be taught the fundamentals of business and finance. My assumption is that in most companies a small number of people truly understand an income or cash flow statement, let alone a balance sheet. Another startling assumption is that most of them do not really care to learn. Your winners do, so hang in there. Few employees comprehend the ramifications of their actions and activities on the financial health of the organization. Break it down to connect the tasks with the numbers you are attempting to impact so that your employees do get it. Demonstrate to them what areas of the various financial statements they can influence by doing their tasks more efficiently, by buying more intelligently, by managing what is important rather than what is familiar or comfortable, by doing the right things that they have control over. Pay attention to what Woody Allen said, "Organized crime in America takes in over $40 billion a year and spends very little on office supplies." What are you spending too much on in your organization? Are your people aware of the impact?

Make available to your employees opportunities for enrolling into in-house or on-campus financial training seminars. Internally, your financial guru can spotlight the areas on the financials that make sense to the individual employees and address what they do at work that would significantly affect the statements. Banks provide classes on financial management. Local colleges offer evening financial curriculum at low tuition rates. There are abundant resources available if you have someone investigate and select. Because you are a business and your scorecard is financial, you had better educate your employees on the business of being in business. Granted not all employees will be interested, but why punish the rest who are by not offering and encouraging participation? Remember keepers want to learn and expand their business acumen. Give them the opportunity. There will be a return.

**Review:** To be a successful and effective leader of a business you must:

1. Remember you are in business to make money.
2. Pound your financial stakes in terra firma.
3. Create your box score.
4. Do not fly blind.
5. Insist upon financial literacy.

**Robust actions to take:**

1. Identify your financial stakes for your organization.

2. Determine the financial indicators in your corporate box score.

3. Select the financial reports that you need. When do you need them? In what form? Who should provide them to you?

4. State how you are going to communicate your financials to your organization. Identify what is going to be communicated.

# 7

## STRATEGY SEVEN:
## Have A Well-Lubricated Reverse Gear

*When the horse is dead, get off.*
—ANONYMOUS

∽

**Keep constant vigilance.**

ANONYMOUS IS RIGHT. However, make sure that your chosen strategic mount has actually rolled over and taken its last gasp breath before you discard it at the local glue factory. As Honest Abe said, "It is not best to swap horses while crossing the river." You can go deep underwater doing that dismount. Leaders should undertake new business strategies only after their current choice has reached its logical and final conclusion. Pay attention to what is or is not working. Do not be so involved in working in your business that you forget to work on the business from the perspective of an external, objective observer rather than an internal, passionate participant.

Remember the last nine words of any dying business are, "This is the way we have always done it." You must examine constantly, explore, and test what, how, and why you are doing what you are doing. If the expense of continuing the activity is not in direct correlation with the profit it contributes, then you must eliminate it, or dumb it down. Whether it hints, whispers, or shouts back at you that something is not working, make intentional, well-considered, and appropriate changes.

While the economy tends to slow down, speed up, and experiences spurts and sputters, the velocity of change continues to accelerate aggressively forward at a rate never before encountered. Jack, when at General Electric, suggested, "When the external rate of change exceeds the internal rate of change, the end is near." You cannot assume that what worked yesterday will work today, tomorrow, or ever again. Constant and vigilant calibration is necessary in today's global and instantly connected business environment.

It is impossible to change a tire tearing down the highway at eighty miles per hour in your turbo-charged convertible with the wind in your face, baseball hat turned backward, and bugs stuck between your teeth. If your wheels are deflating or have gone completely flat, you should pull over and put on a new tire or pump fresh air into the old one. What is your air gauge telling you?

The same approach applies when at the wheel of a stalled or out-of-control business heading toward an unanticipated ditch, or not firing on all cylinders. Put on the brakes, slow down, and come to a controlled stop. Deliberately, carefully, with all your senses on full alert, select the reverse gear and ease the business back to disengage and free yourself from the collision. Unbuckle and step out of whatever you are driving and position yourself so that you can view the situation from another perspective and intelligently explore what caused the wreck rather than settling for a quick snapshot of the accident. You cannot evaluate the situation when you are inside the yellow crime scene tape. You do not want to look down on the pavement and see a chalk silhouette of your business. It would be inappropriate, foolish, and irresponsible to stubbornly roar on, engine racing, wind again in your face, white knuckling forward when the evidence presenting itself through the windshield, in full living color, suggests an immediate pit stop. You are not an all-terrain vehicle. Be resilient, not persistent.

Author Stephen Covey suggests, "Live out of your imagination, not your history." In business, unlike with people, the past is not always the best predictor of future, guaranteed success. Remember Xerox, IBM, Eastman Kodak, and Polaroid. These international behemoths hit the skids hard in the 1990s as they ignored penetration into their traditional markets by competitors that were not the usual suspects. The new players were simply discounted and dismissed. Three out of the four global giants recovered because of deep pockets and sustaining power. Could you and your business absorb a below-the-belt blow that devastating? Probably not. Learn this lesson. Do not become arrogant and fall in love with what you believe is your inherent right to be number one with your customers and that your well-established, traditional competitive edge will last forever. If your focus is on keeping your edge razor-sharp by using that familiar back and forth stroke on the same timeworn leather strap, it just may turn against you one day and slit your self-serving throat. Sir Winston Churchill said, "However beautiful the strategy, you should occasionally look at the results." That is a good and appropriate idea. Are you doing it?

## Hire and train strategic thinkers.

Strategically moving your business forward is an all-consuming and encompassing task. You cannot do this alone. You need to team internally with your version of what Rudyard Kipling identifies as his "six honest men."

> *I keep six honest men*
> *(they taught me all I knew);*
> *Their names are What and Why and When*
> *And How and Where and Who.*

—from *The Elephant's Child*

Strategic thinking and deliberate intelligent application focuses primarily on one of the six honest men, Mr. **How.** When you think of strategy, think "How am I going to accomplish something? How am I going to come to market? How am I going to compete with the behemoths? How is this organization going to become unstuck?" In the answer lies the strategy. Eventually, all the other honest men, where, what, why, when, and who join in and play their cameo roles in creating and implementing the plan.

Do you have among your employees a Mr. **Who** that can intelligently, consistently, and effectively team with you to determine how you are going to strategically accelerate your organization toward your vision? Experience unfortunately suggests that you probably do not. Many of you do not have an internal human inventory of well-educated, seasoned, perceptive, experienced MBAs at your disposal to strategize your next move. Business author Jim Collins anchors the need to always be seeking and upgrading your talent by suggesting, "Great vision without great people is irrelevant."

Mr. **When** enters the scene as the immediate response to identified problems or the initiating of appropriate changes. Do not procrastinate. Be decisive. You must be action-oriented and impatient.

Mr. **What** is simply the goals and the vision that you are driving the organization toward.

Mr. **Why** is the justification of whatever you are implementing, the intention motivating you to accomplish something. It needs to be appropriate and focused on doing the right things.

Mr. **Where** is whatever market segment you are attempting to penetrate. It may be geographical or vertical but it needs to be clearly defined.

Jeff Bezos, Founder and CEO of Amazon.com said, "When a company is very small, you focus on the **who**, the **what**, and the **how**. When it was just me, I focused on all three. Over time you give up on the how, then you give up on the what and focus on the who." What are you doing to give up all of the roles that you once assumed so that you can step into your most appropriate slot on the organization chart and do what you are supposed to do?

Most companies that I have worked with create and organize themselves in a silo structure relative to the management level on the organization chart. You have a definitive silo where the beans are counted, another silo for sales and marketing, one for operations to maneuver around in, and on and on down the horizontal and vertical lines, you classify specific functions and hire capable captains to perform within their defined boundaries and job descriptions.

Seldom do the captains assist you in strategizing at the same level that the MBAs do at Fortune 500 companies. Seldom do they possess the perspective of an owner, CEO, or are they able to look down at the business from a 30,000-foot elevation overview. You cannot find fault with that because you did not hire them to fulfill that strategic role. They are mired in their own fishbowl swimming about in their own familiar water doing what is comfortable, known, and predictable. You need to change this.

Not to worry. My most forward-thinking, successful CEO clients partially overcame this situation by executing the following strategy regarding their direct reports. Classify your managers into the following four categories.

**Category one—the stars:** Evaluate your roster and select those that have demonstrated the most consistent ability in assisting you to move the organization forward strategically. Single them out and inform them of their expanded role. They are allowed to sit with you at the strategic planning conference table and suggest appropriate strategic input relative to leading the business, not just managing their particular silo. Provide them adequate leadership and strategic training. Challenge them to reach their Peter Principle, then push them to go one rung higher, then one more. Help them discover their ceiling. Teach them what you know (you know a lot) that propelled you to the chair that you are sitting in.

As a leader, you are obligated to pay special attention and to continue to further develop your stars. Remember to spend 80 percent of your time developing your top 20 percent. Do not reverse this. If you cannot identify anyone to sit with you, you are probably already upside down in the ditch, wheels spinning, or approaching terminal burnout because you are doing it all yourself, working continually on the same familiar unresolved issues. You might consider selling the business, doing something that you really enjoy, and getting your life back in some semblance of balance.

**Category two—the rising stars:** For those employees on the organization chart who show promise, untapped potential and keen interest, provide them specific training, mentoring, coaching, role modeling, and the occasional opportunity to participate strategically with you and the chosen stars. Design a professional internal and external development program to accelerate them to stardom. They are your winners-in-waiting.

You may have a future star being blocked in a silo by a category four manager. That does happen. Evaluate the situation and if appropriate, terminate that manager. The winners-in-waiting should be given the opportunity to strut their stuff and demonstrate what they are capable of doing. You must pay close attention to this group for they are your future.

**Category three—the worker bees:** These are the salt-of-the-earth, the vanilla, the reliable, the good, solid, stable, foundational managers and their reports who show up everyday, give you their best, do not complain, and live the company values even when nobody is watching. Thank goodness for them. Give them a raise when appropriate.

Spend some time with them. Thank them for their contribution and acknowledge their accomplishments. They will appreciate your interest.

**Category four—the black holes:** For those managers that historically display limited ability or interest and are still standing patiently in line collecting your company welfare check, have HR escort them to the nearest exit and wish them and their new employer well. They are a drain on your net worth, equity, and compensation package. Are you finally getting the point that what I am relentlessly preaching is the creation and protection of your financial security?

Replace the black hole slackers with those that demonstrate through past, validated experience, the ability to think strategically and to perform a designated function in the organization at an elevated level. You need to recruit and interview for these traits.

Upgrading the talent within the silos at every opportunity is essential and keeps you in the present and future game where you have chosen to compete. You had better have a proactive talent search and a defined process to evaluate quickly the people who show up at your door.

The role of a strategic thinking management team and their designated leader is to intelligently strategize and implement the following four activities:

- **Evaluate continually the present and future needs of your customers.**

- **Satisfy those needs profitably.**

- **Monitor continually your competition.**

- **Keep your competitive advantage appropriate.**

## Evaluate continually the present and future needs of your customer.

I intentionally chose "needs" not "wants." If you attempt to provide your customers with all that they want, they will pick you clean and you will value-add yourself right out of a once-profitable business and wonder, in the name of a completely satisfied customer, what in the world happened. "I thought I was doing things right." Well you were but you should have been doing the right things. You do not have to be everything to all people, at all times, under all conditions. Specialize. Do not be run ragged, or held hostage, by your highest volume and loudest customers. Let other suppliers provide your customers their specialties. Be willing to say "no" and do not always assume that your most vocal and largest customer has the most credibility.

You need to stick consistently with what you do best and continue to improve that specific offering. When you completely turnkey your product, you tend to dilute your core competency, send unnecessary dollars down the toilet, and lose sight and grasp of your expertise.

Occasionally, it is a good idea to actually ask your customer, "Do you value all that we are providing, and is it helping you and your business be successful?" That should be a CEO-to-CEO continual conversation. Become the Chief Sales Officer along with being the CEO. You might be astounded to hear, "This is all very nice, but what we would really like is a lower price per unit and you can keep all the value-added offerings that are increasing your costs that I suspect you are now passing on to me. We simply do not value it as much as you do." Ask the customer; now that is an interesting concept. In any CEO-to-CEO sales call, it is essential that you discuss how doing business with you and your company will help the buyer:

- **grow his/her company.**

- **reduce costs.**

- **become more profitable.**

If you, as CEO of your company, can provide those three outcomes to your CEO buyer, you have a running start at consummating a deal. Years ago when I was selling for Xerox, I sold features and benefits. I would do it differently today and enter into a "business-speak" conversation with the prospective customer. Features and benefits are mildly interesting compared to a sound business proposition that demonstrates how using my products will improve my client's business. Remember the words of comedian Bill Cosby who said, "I don't know the key to success, but the key to failure is trying to please everybody."

The majority of the time, companies focus on meeting and understanding the present needs of their customers because that provides the constant river of cash required to keep the doors open. With their noses to the grindstone and attention riveted upon getting the next order completed and shipped, they often lose sight of the future and the opportunity to be at the intersection when a new offering and their customer's unique needs simultaneously engage.

Even if you have limited resources, you are still able to collect data that when gathered and analyzed will provide you with an educated peek into your customer's future needs. Try the following:

- Always debrief your salespeople when they come in from the cold.

- Make CEO-to-CEO sales calls on your best customers.

- Check out your customer and competitors' websites.

- Attend customer and your industry trade shows.

- Gather all employees who interact with your customers and brainstorm new and innovative ways you can improve the relationships.

- Subscribe to and read your market's publications, looking for trends.

- Create a focus group with your best customers and ask them what they need from you.

- Warehouse all this information, and with objective external input, analyze the data.

All of these activities are minimal cost items providing low-hanging fruit for you to pick, digest, and make appropriate choices regarding your customer's needs and direction. Do something. Do not be squandering your time hanging out on some familiar street corner waiting for your market to sucker punch you squarely on your nose because you are too busy, looking one inch in front of you, doing what you have always done in the manner that you have always done it. Does this make sense?

One does not have to go back too far in history to see how quickly markets can change; needs are identified, strategies evolved, and new and existing customers are rapidly satisfied by "unusual suspects."

In the past, the majority of books were purchased primarily through local corner bookstores. The owners and operators of those businesses provided somewhat limited inventories, priced their products competitively, and developed a loyal customer base. The businesses were doing fine. They were not setting the world on fire, but they were producing moderate profits and satisfying the needs of a defined market of book buyers. The owners and operators also had unconsciously and collectively reached over and pressed the snooze button. What about the future?

Some seemingly smart people noticed that a large population of consumers was wandering about in huge cavernous concrete boxes, with massive parking lots, purchasing all types of merchandise in mammoth volumes. Boxes of Tylenol were seen roped onto the tops of automobiles. A one-year supply of toilet paper was being sandwiched between hyperactive, suburban preschoolers in the backseats of Ford Expeditions.

Why not books? Enter Borders, Barnes & Noble, and others. Instantly, some of the corner bookstores toppled off the radar screen. These superstores strutted around with new bricks and mortar, unlimited inventory, Starbucks coffee, low everyday pricing, anchor tenant status, elaborate branding strategies, and bulging budgets. They were feeling good about penetrating this market with a unique delivery channel that met the needs of a growing, interested, and consuming market. They had implemented successfully their Wall Street business plan. What about the future?

Other intelligent folks noticed that there was a large and growing population of consumers that were comfortable and familiar with buying a variety of merchandise online. Why not books? Enter Amazon and diminishing market share for the big boxes and corner bookstores. Amazon went global the instant they went into business. That was hardly fair, traditional, or expected.

Spending enormous sums of investor money on marketing a limited number of products, the brain trust at Amazon concluded that if they continued on that path, it would lead to one of those nasty train wrecks. Resetting their strategy, they noticed that they had a gazillion credit card numbers, e-mail addresses, and a channel process that was proven successful. Not a bad formula for mass merchandising a variety of products and positioning themselves as an online shopping mall. Things change and you need to change with them at the same or at an accelerated rate. What about the future?

All of this happened quickly and with little advance warning. As you read this book, brilliant people with deep pockets are spending time, energy, and money figuring out the next opportunity to satisfy an emerging, voracious market. You may be the bull's-eye in their laser-focused, high-powered arsenal. Maybe you could sell your business to them?

You are now competing in a rapidly changing and evolving world. Your advantage is your nimbleness and your ability to act upon information quickly. You have the ability to walk outside your office and shout at full volume to your stars, "left," and the organization can, and perhaps will, move in that direction without passing through hoops of meetings, board approval, and volumes of data. Keep your eye on the future and do your best to figure out how you are going to participate profitably in satisfying the present and future needs of your customers.

## Satisfy your customer's needs profitably.

Unless you are burning an endless supply of investor money, your financial well is only so deep and can quickly run dry if you are not paying attention to your numbers. You cannot afford to be fiscally promiscuous by ignoring your own monetary needs in an effort to satisfy a demanding customer who will drop you like a hot, glowing coal the moment a competitor comes in with a lower price per unit. Yes, you can build firewalls around the account by extraordinary service, on-time deliveries, face-to-face interaction, and all the rest. The fact remains that all customers, at some point in their life cycle, are temporary due to the significance of the box score and the inevitable and eventual fate of all products being coldly tossed into the commodity bin where price rules. Ultimately, the numbers drive nearly all business decisions and relationships.

There will be times when you are forced to sacrifice profits in the name of growing your business and investing for the future, but be prudent. I had a client in the high-end, wood frame, window business. Vern had successfully and with great care shepherded a family business into its third generation. Statistically that is quite an accomplishment. While at the helm, he grew the top and bottom line and developed a well-earned reputation with local builders and distributors as a quality, dependable, branded supplier. In an effort to expand his business and diversify his offering, he diluted his traditional wood-framed window business by venturing into manufacturing vinyl-framed windows. At the time, with what he knew, it seemed like a good, intelligent strategy. The product was appealing to builders because of its shelf life and cost. He invested considerable cash in new, state-of-the-art manufacturing equipment, hired additional employees to produce the product, and diverted his and the company's focus to recruiting and securing fresh customers.

Vern went fishing, set the hook, and landed a promising new customer who was a demanding, national chain, big box, home improvement retail store. This was virgin and exciting territory. To meet the customer's needs of high volume, low price, and distribution to multiple locations, he found himself compromising his business model and placing in harm's way the consistent profits and focus that his traditional products had provided historically. He felt like a puppet on a short string dancing to the unpredictable and unfamiliar whims, needs, and wants of an uncaring giant. It was an impending train wreck in the making.

After considerable anguish and experiencing further compression of his margins, Vern pulled the plug on his newest, most prestigious customer and began to pay more attention to manufacturing his core products and selling to established and familiar customers. He once again returned to the dance floor and waltzed primarily with the girl he brought to the dance.

At times, you need to muster up the courage to fire customers because they are not always right and not always right for you. You do not need nor deserve the chronic headache that accompanies working with difficult, high maintenance, unlimited stamina, customers. This is not always easy to do because you rationalize why you continue to keep them.

- ◆ They contribute to overhead coverage.

- ◆ They have been loyal through hard times.

- ◆ Your relationship goes beyond business.

- ◆ You do not know if you can replace them.

- ◆ And many others.

When all is said and done, if the time spent on them is not related directly to their contribution to your profitability, it is time to cut them loose and focus on those customers who do. Ask your profitable customers for more business. You are already in the door and generating revenues. These existing customer expansions are easy picking and not to be overlooked.

Vern continues to produce the vinyl window frames but now sells them to customers who will negotiate and agree to a fair and equitable price at a fair and equitable margin. He did the right thing.

## Monitor your competition.

If you are selling into a viable market and knocking down sizable profits, your success is going to draw attention, and someone is going to notice. Hello competition. Like bears to a honey jar, you will be discovered and others will attempt to penetrate your playpen, take away market share, and slice and dice your margins. Pay attention to how these players come to your market. You should welcome and bless fair competition. When you witness a competitor derailing your plans or outperforming you and your people, it is an invitation to wake up, place complacency aside, and explore the infinite possibilities before you.

As Mario Puzo's Godfather said, "Keep your friends close but keep your enemies closer." The bullet that can kill you is usually the one you do not see being fired from a sniper's nest.

Get your antennas telescoped skyward, turn your radar on to sweep the horizon, calibrate your GPS system, and analyze the data. It is much easier and less costly to imitate rather than to initiate. It is much more effective to strategize defensive and offensive maneuvers once you know your enemy, where they are, and how they operate.

Sleuth around and gather as much "intel" as you can. Turn your marketing people into Chief Intelligence Officers. Copy what works for your competition and put your own spin on their process that fits with how you like to do business. I do not believe in the adage, "If we just keep focused on what we do well, to heck with the others guys, everything will work out." You are not the only leader who has found success and who can implement innovative ideas. Sam Walton, founder of WalMart said, "Most everything I have done I've copied from someone else." He was fairly successful, why not you?

## Keep your competitive advantage appropriate.

Bruce Henderson, founder of the Boston Consulting Group, shares his thoughts on competitive advantage in a 1989 *Harvard Business Review* article. Henderson writes,

*Strategy is a deliberate search for a plan of action that will develop a business' competitive advantage and compound it. For any company the search is an interactive process that begins with recognition of where you are and what you have now. Your most dangerous competitors are those that are most like you. The differences between you and your competitors are the basis of your advantage. If you are in business and self-supporting, you already have some kind of competitive advantage no matter how small or subtle. Otherwise, you would have gradually lost customers faster than you gained them. The objective is to enlarge the scope of the advantage which can only happen at someone else's expense.*

And I say, "Amen, and do not fall in love with it."

Ben Franklin proposed that, "It is hard for an empty bag to stand upright." Your current competitive advantage had better have some relevance and substance to it or you are history. If your proposition is failing, then change it. Ed Zander, CEO of Motorola, says, "You've got to take big swings once in a while…You've got to set a course and not be afraid to make a mistake." No amount of money, brilliant execution, advertising, employee perks, or anything else is going to support or rescue an inappropriate and weak business proposition. Keep this advantage singular so you can keep it sharp and focus your resources on what is vital and essential to your success.

Make it highly visible to the organization so it is understood thoroughly and available to refine consciously. Your competitive advantage should inspire you and the organization to exceed all previous expectations. It should motivate customers to continue to do business with you. It should attract prospects to join you on your journey. It should be a beacon for talented people to climb on board. It should be a rail to ride to your explicit vision.

This advantage should leapfrog you over competitors and enable the business to leap tall buildings with a single bound instead of incrementally grinding it out. A compelling, competitive advantage should accelerate your company to being a market leader, one viewed by your peers as the best and the only enterprise that they should engage in a business relationship.

**Review:** To be a successful and effective leader of a business you must:

1. Keep constant vigilance.
2. Hire and train strategic thinkers.
3. Evaluate continually the present and future needs of your customers.
4. Satisfy your customer's needs profitably.
5. Monitor your competition.
6. Keep your competitive advantage appropriate.

**Robust actions to take:**

1. **What** are trying to accomplish in your business?

2. **Why** are you trying to accomplish this?

3. **When** do you want this completed?

4. **How** are you going to do this?

5. **Who** is your most feared competitor?

6. **What** is your competitive edge over this competitor?

# EPILOGUE

*"There is no training to be a CEO;*
*it's an extraordinary thing."*
—GERALD LEVIN

KENNETH W. FREEMAN, CEO of Quest Diagnostics says, "Being a CEO is not a birthright, it's a privilege." You, fortunately, are one of the privileged few. Congratulations. After finishing this epilogue, you can put the book down, cap the colored highlighters, turn off your laptop, pour yourself a glass of that Bordeaux, lean back in the recliner and reflect on what you have accomplished and then decide what needs to happen next. Fortunately, there is always a "next" being a successful leader of an organization. This propels you into a state of aliveness and becomingness. That is a good thing. Participate actively in your evolution.

It is my hope that the seven strategies resonate with you and that you will implement all seven to the maximum as you continue on your individual journey. Remember what I said about not discounting this material because it may appear to you to be fundamentally too simple and much too obvious. Technology author E. F. Schumaker suggests, "Any intelligent fool can make things bigger, more complex, and more violent. It takes a touch of genius—and a lot of courage—to move in the opposite direction." To assist you in moving toward simplicity and increased effectiveness there is one more exercise for you to complete. Oh, you may finish the wine first. You deserve to pamper yourself for a few more minutes.

Please evaluate yourself on a scale of 1 to 10 on the seven strategies. Circle your score. One (1) is poor and ten (10) is excellent. Being excellent is a good thing.

## BEING AUTHENTIC

1    2    3    4    5    6    7    (8)    9    10

*Robust actions I need to take to be a 10.*

Example:

| ROBUST ACTION | BY WHEN | RESOURCES | MEASUREMENT | NOTES |
|---|---|---|---|---|
| 1. *Search the internet for self-actualization books and seminars* | *During first quarter 2005* | *Internet and Amazon.com* | *Read at least two books and attend one seminar by 3/31/05* | *I feel good about this decision* |

## BEING AUTHENTIC

1   2   3   4   5   6   7   8   9   10

*Robust actions I need to take to be a 10.*

| ROBUST ACTION | BY WHEN | RESOURCES | MEASUREMENT | NOTES |
|---|---|---|---|---|
| 1. | | | | |
| 2. | | | | |
| 3. | | | | |
| 4. | | | | |
| 5. | | | | |

## TAKING CARE OF MYSELF

1   2   3   4   5   6   7   8   9   10

*Robust actions I need to take to be a 10.*

| ROBUST ACTION | BY WHEN | RESOURCES | MEASUREMENT | NOTES |
|---|---|---|---|---|
| 1. | | | | |
| 2. | | | | |
| 3. | | | | |
| 4. | | | | |
| 5. | | | | |

## BEING A LEADER

### 1  2  3  4  5  6  7  8  9  10

*Robust actions I need to take to be a 10.*

| ROBUST ACTION | BY WHEN | RESOURCES | MEASUREMENT | NOTES |
|---|---|---|---|---|
| 1. | | | | |
| 2. | | | | |
| 3. | | | | |
| 4. | | | | |
| 5. | | | | |

## BEING RESILIENT

### 1  2  3  4  5  6  7  8  9  10

*Robust actions I need to take to be a 10.*

| ROBUST ACTION | BY WHEN | RESOURCES | MEASUREMENT | NOTES |
|---|---|---|---|---|
| 1. | | | | |
| 2. | | | | |
| 3. | | | | |
| 4. | | | | |
| 5. | | | | |

## UPGRADING MY TALENT

1   2   3   4   5   6   7   8   9   10

*Robust actions I need to take to be a 10.*

| ROBUST ACTION | BY WHEN | RESOURCES | MEASUREMENT | NOTES |
|---|---|---|---|---|
| 1. | | | | |
| 2. | | | | |
| 3. | | | | |
| 4. | | | | |
| 5. | | | | |

## UNDERSTANDING MY NUMBERS

1   2   3   4   5   6   7   8   9   10

*Robust actions I need to take to be a 10.*

| ROBUST ACTION | BY WHEN | RESOURCES | MEASUREMENT | NOTES |
|---|---|---|---|---|
| 1. | | | | |
| 2. | | | | |
| 3. | | | | |
| 4. | | | | |
| 5. | | | | |

## KEEPING MY EDGE SHARP

### 1   2   3   4   5   6   7   8   9   10

*Robust actions I need to take to be a 10.*

| ROBUST ACTION | BY WHEN | RESOURCES | MEASUREMENT | NOTES |
|---|---|---|---|---|
| 1. | | | | |
| 2. | | | | |
| 3. | | | | |
| 4. | | | | |
| 5. | | | | |

I hope that while reading this book, you were laughing, thinking, and shedding a few tears. I did all three while writing.

Remember the words of Harrison Ford and Jim Valvano, "Stay on the bus" and "Do not give up." You deserve the very best in life. Go for it. I have enjoyed my time with you and hope that you have had a similar experience.

Warm regards,

*Ole*

**OLE CARLSON**, author, corporate trainer, strategic planning consultant, and keynote speaker, has spoken to CEO audiences in North America, The United Kingdom, Europe, and Australia, on corporate leadership, personal growth, and strategic planning. In 1999, Ole was recognized as one of Australia's top international business speakers and has received awards and recognition for his presentations by various CEO organizations in the United States and the United Kingdom.

He has been a lead trainer for several transformational seminars, served as a CEO coach, group facilitator, and a corporate trainer for a San Diego-based international leader of CEO forums. His strategic planning clients range from small start-ups to international New York security exchanges.

A graduate of the University of Washington, Ole and his wife Sue Ann, reside in La Quinta, California and can be reached at:

Web site: influencemany.com
E-mail: ole@influencemany.com
sa@influencemany.com

NOTES

## NOTES

# NOTES

# NOTES